In *From Trauma to Trust*, Jan shows us the toll unremembered trauma takes on our souls, the courage it takes to start to face it, and how faith can be healing instead of harmful. Her memoir is more than just memories, it is a guide and a beacon of hope for people on their own journeys to heal.

Kimberley L. Benton, Psy.D.

"I wish I had a protector so I could grow a new hard shell" is voiced by Jan in this remarkably painful and liberating memoir. The author invites us into an enriched life, one that was fought for at many junctures. As an only child, she remembers every important adult figure in her life. She tells the truth, the ugly, and beautiful all mixed in together. To say that she survived in a dysfunctional family is an understatement. The author found purpose and hope through nurture in the church, her schools, and her friends. She was wrapped all along in a faith community that kept her safe and valued. As a United Methodist Campus Minister, she excelled, using her own life script as a way to be present in every circumstance to diverse students in their own explorations and crises. What emerged over decades is the story of a strong, resilient, determined, and caring woman who finally can embrace herself fully. In her words, all she ever wanted was "Wanting to be Found. Needing to feel Loved." I loved this book and the woman who emerged in its telling. The courage it took to write it and offer it to others is absolutely inspiring.

Charlene P. Kammerer<br>Bishop, The United Methodist Church, retired

JAN RIVERO

# From Trauma to Trust

**A SPIRITUAL JOURNEY**

© 2025
Published in the United States by Nurturing Faith, Macon, GA.
Nurturing Faith is a book imprint of Good Faith Media (goodfaithmedia.org).
Library of Congress Cataloging-in-Publication Data is available.

ISBN:978-1-63528-261-0

All rights reserved. Printed in the United States of America.
Scriptures taken from the New Revised Standard Version Bible, copyright © 1989, National Council of the Churches of Christ in the United States of America. Used by permission. All rights reserved worldwide.

*For*
*Alayna, Adelyn and Insley*

*"God is always at home.
It is we who have gone out for a walk."
Meister Eckhart*

# PROLOGUE

My feet were like lead the day I walked out of my campus ministry office in Chapel Hill for the last time. It was a classic Tarheel summer day. Heavy with humidity, the air sagged like wet laundry on a clothesline and felt sticky on my cool skin. It was June; I should not have expected different weather. Still, it added weight to my already sinking spirit.

My rewarding work with students, faculty, and staff was complete. I loved this ministry and often told others I had the best job in the world. Departing was bittersweet after twelve years of meaningful ministry. To stem my sadness, I reminded myself my work had mattered—even made a difference. I journeyed with students in their trauma and shepherded them in their spiritual and personal growth. With faculty, I provided service-learning opportunities to enrich students' academic experiences. With student affairs staff and in partnership with other campus ministry colleagues, I helped encourage a healthy environment for the development of the whole student. I contributed to the field of ministry in higher education at the national and international levels, led workshops on student leadership at conferences, and held positions on campus ministry boards. My tenure had borne good fruit.

This leave-taking carried with it the odd sensation that I had been self-defrocked (metaphorically, that is), professionally disrobed. Campus ministry had been my call and identity for over twenty years. My professional destination was a mystery, but I knew now was the time. I could feel myself aging out. The language and music of students was foreign to me now. I was their parents' age. It was time to move on. So, I did. The problem was I landed on an uncharted path with no compass to guide me.

*What will I do with myself? What happens now that I have no goals?*

For the first time in my life, I was free-floating. Ungrounded. Without purpose. I was an inner tube on a river headed downstream, oblivious to the rapids ahead.

I considered writing a devotional book: gathering up reflections on my encounters with the Holy on my grandparents' farm on the Eastern Shore of Virginia. Those stories called to me now as if they longed to be told.

But when I tried to put words on paper, it proved more painful than giving birth. No amount of pushing my pen across the page produced a coherent thought. Despite my best efforts, that baby was not ready to be born. My spirit resisted. So, I shoved the idea back into my desk drawer and took a job with a non-profit organization working to alleviate world hunger. Leveraging the relationships I had developed in higher education, I cultivated partnerships to raise awareness about hunger on campuses nationwide. It was good work, but the organization functioned like a boys' club and my efforts were questioned if not thwarted. It took about thirty months for me to realize that my best gifts were being wasted. I began to sense a call to return to parish ministry, to teach and preach and pastor, to serve one more congregation before retirement. I sent my vestments to the dry cleaners, and we packed up the house and moved to Charlottesville, Virginia, where I served a university church for three years. Following the Unite the Right Rally in 2017, though, preaching presented a prophetic challenge that I knew was unsustainable, so I decided to join Jeffrey, my partner of twenty-three years, in retirement.

We moved into a new home in August 2019. On our first morning in the house, Jeffrey rested on a couch recovering from minor surgery. I worked in the kitchen nearby, unpacking the large, brown cardboard boxes labeled KITCHEN. Plates, bowls, mugs, and platters were arranged with care in the cabinet next to the ovens. As I organized the drawer next to the refrigerator with paring knives, can openers, whisks, and wooden spoons, there came a sudden, unexpected crash on the roof. Thor's hammer dropped through the ceiling and landed at my feet.

In Norse mythology, Thor is a larger-than-life character with a massive, heavy hammer, which he uses as a weapon of destruction and, in other contexts, to provide divine blessing. In contemporary mythology, Thor, the Marvel superhero, is played by Chris Hemsworth, who uses his hammer to destroy evil and restore good. Despite my Swedish heritage, I imagined the modern-day superhero appearing in my kitchen at any second. But what alarmed me was not the hammer at my feet. What grabbed my attention was the yellow sticky note attached to it. The note read, "Book Title: Toxicology Report."

*Oh. My. God!*

A rational human might have taken time to consider what had happened, but I was looking around for Chris Hemsworth. As my head cleared, I realized my imagination was playing games with me. Moving is exhausting, after all. I looked up and saw the ceiling was intact. There was no damage, no chunks of drywall on the floor, and no dust swirling in the aftermath. No hammer. No sticky note. Sadly, there was also no Chris Hemsworth.

One thing had changed, however. A gauntlet had landed at my feet. To run the gauntlet, or "gatlopp" in ancient Sweden, was to traverse a military passage while being struck by clubs, heavy ropes, or straps. This moment challenged me to tell the truth, to face the daunting task of telling my whole story. My grandparents' farm had given me the happiest chapters of my childhood, but that was less than half of my story. The rest was unsavory and unhappy—chapters too painful to admit to myself. The imaginary sticky note invited me to take a different path, explore my pain, make sense of it, and put it to rest. I knew it would not be easy, gentle, or fun—this gauntlet had the potential to be brutal.

*Do I dare say "yes" to this?*

The painful parts of my story were tucked away, buried, and covered with denial decades before. They were swallowed up by thick, gooey, dark mud, sunken in the creek bed for years.

*Do I want to dredge them up? Am I asking for trouble?*

From a young age, I protected this burial ground. Now, my past begged for fresh air. Flashbacks were directing me back to myself, and I needed to embrace them.

Eight months later, as COVID infected and shut down the globe, I sat at my desk and looked out the window toward the mountain ridge. The naked skeletons of tree trunks showed signs of spring. Soon, the hillside would be a raiment of green. I picked up my pen and willed my memories to claim me so this might become a devotional after all—a testament to the mysterious ways God invites us to wholeness.

# CHAPTER 1

## September 1953

The first time I met my grandparents, it might have happened like this.

Emily and Herman climbed the stairs to the third floor of Doctor's Hospital in Flushing, New York. They were uncharacteristically somber, especially considering they were there to welcome their third grandchild, their daughter's first baby. It could have been a celebratory day, but Emily did not see it that way. Instead, she felt as though the vase of pink fairy roses in her hands held the weight of the world. They tiptoed into their daughter's room to find the infant in her mother's arms. The baby's father sat at the bedside. His large smile and wide eyes radiated pride and adoration.

Emily mustered the smallest smile. Her cheeks trembled as she struggled to hide her disdain for this unholy situation. She asked the safe question, "What's her name?"

"She doesn't have one yet," Lolly responded, her voice weak as she recovered from a long and painful labor. She was baptized as Laura, but everyone called her Lolly.

I was supposed to be a boy. Mom and Dad were prepared to call me Mark, but they had not entertained the possibility I might be a girl. They were so sure I was a boy they never considered girls' names. In those days, mothers and newborns stayed in the hospital for several days, so by the time Mom and I were ready to go home, I had a name as beautiful and rhythmic as a Spanish flamenco. They chose a middle name to honor both of my grandmothers, which added depth of meaning to my identity. Problem solved! Except for the fact Mom and Dad did not want to call me Janice or Maria. They called me BJ, short for Baby Janice.

My name mattered little, if at all, to Emily. What troubled her was her son-in-law. Emily had been raised in a strict, conservative Christian home by a father who had immigrated from Denmark. He was a holy roller who prohibited music, dancing, playing cards, and (as one would expect) smoking or drinking any form of alcohol. Her mother, a Swedish immigrant, was a dutiful wife and mother. So, Emily held tight to solid values and hard and fast biblically-based rules. When I say tight, I mean vice-grip tight. Her world was binary. It was rare for her to waver or change her mind. Compromise and negotiation seemed unfamiliar to her.

Her son-in-law, my father, whom everyone called Riv, flew in the face of all she stood for. He had been raised Catholic, but that was the least of her qualms. She bristled at his ethnicity as a Venezuelan immigrant and fretted that her grandchildren would be brown. The fifteen-year age difference between him and Lolly troubled her too. But what bothered her most was he had been married twice before. He was twice divorced with two daughters—one from each marriage. And now, with his third wife he has a third daughter.

Emily could not fathom why, in the name of everything holy, her daughter had married him. She had raised Lolly as she had been raised, with strict rules and without liberal permissions. All the evidence suggested that Emily and Herman had done an excellent job. Lolly was brilliant. She excelled academically. She  graduated from high school at sixteen and college at twenty. She was a championship archer. She won competitions at the local and state levels and competed at the 1939 New York World's Fair. But she was devastated when her fiancé went to war in Europe and did not return home. Emily could not fix her daughter's grief. Instead, the relationship between mother and daughter became co-dependent. To protect Lolly from more pain, Emily took control of her life. Lolly was too raw not to let her. That is, until she met and married Riv.

And now, there they were, all together, to welcome the newest family member. It was never Emily's style to bite her lip or keep her judgments to herself, but for Lolly's sake and to keep the peace, she did her best to be pleasant. She cooed and ga-ga-ed and tickled my chin. But she was not happy.

Days later, when Emily acquiesced and allowed her new granddaughter's name to sink in, she embraced it, but not without letting Lolly know what she thought of the nickname. "BJ? Phooey!" she said—the closest thing to a cuss word she ever allowed to cross her lips.

She refused to call me BJ and called me Janice until the day she died. It was fine with me. I never liked the nickname and answered to it because I did not know better. When I started school, I realized it was dismissive—I was no longer a baby. And the older I got, the more inappropriate it was. Hearing Mom or Dad yell "BJ!" felt like walking into a giant cobweb that clung to all of me, too gluey to brush off.

I tried to break them of the habit. "Call me Adele." The name of a girl in my class.

They laughed.

"Don't call me BJ!" I yelled on another occasion.

"What shall we call you then?" Dad's voice taunted me.

"Marsha. Nancy. I don't care. Any name but BJ!"

At last, when they realized I was not about to give up, they honored my request—as best they could. Mom called me "dearie" or "sweetie." Both were more acceptable. Dad called me "kitten." That just felt creepy.

*What is wrong with my name? Why can you not just respect me and my wishes?*

# CHAPTER 2

Before Jeffrey and I moved to Chapel Hill in 1998, I pulled from the attic a box of old movies and pictures. The movie reels were in old gray metal tins. The films of my childhood were grainy with black splotches, and they glitched as they ran through the projector. There were black and white photos, mostly of people I did not recognize, and a few with relatives whom I did. One photo was of Dad: his toothy grin sparkled as he squinted in the sunlight and cradled me in his arms. I was about five months old, in a white onesie and bonnet, chewing on a rubber Bugs Bunny. Together, we stood on the grainy gray sand beach of the Shark River in front of a backdrop of tall pine trees that obscured our tiny cabin. The river water was dark, almost black as if it was holding fast to the secrets of what flowed below the surface. Two years after the photo was taken, my parents left the beach cottage in the woods on the bluff that rose up from the river. We moved to a new house in a new neighborhood next to a new golf course. We still lived in New Jersey, but this new location made Dad's commute to work more convenient.

Our house on Golf Street was a pale-yellow California ranch-style house with a two-car garage, a full basement, and a flat roof. It sat atop a hill at the end of a street stub and it checked off one of the boxes on Dad's "must have" list to reach the American dream. Like many houses in the neighborhood, it had three bedrooms, one-and-a-half baths, green linoleum on the kitchen floor, and cream-colored Formica countertops.

Mom's dark brown Gabler baby grand piano and bench commanded the living room. It was not a purchase she intended to make. After she graduated from college, Lolly moved home with her parents and worked for a company that supported the war. Without rent to pay, she saved enough money to buy a car. But when she amassed the cash for the purchase, her mother would not allow her to do so. She was not going to leave that money in the

bank, and instead of a car, Lolly bought a piano. Ten years later, that piano—the accidental addition—sat in the living room corner like a king on a throne in front of the picture window. During the years of presidential elections, Mom lowered the piano top, and it became the display area for her inherited collection of elephants—over two hundred of them in all sizes, colors, and mediums. Otherwise, the instrument sat dormant. I never saw Mom sit on the bench and I never heard her play a note—not once.

*Why do you have a baby grand piano if you don't play it?*

Next to the piano, Dad built a large, semi-circle-shaped planter. Mom filled it with split-leaf philodendrons. It might have been unremarkable, except Dad screwed small cup hooks into the ceiling and dropped strings from them so the plants could wind their tendrils to the top. Cue the toucan or the marmoset. Either would have been at home in that small jungle.

Beyond the living room was a screen porch. Dad enclosed and converted it into a study and furnished it with a black and white chair and desk. A two-shelved wooden case in the corner was home to the thick and heavy twenty-four-volume Encyclopedia Britannica. Three extended shelves filled with volumes of books hung over his desk. Time-Life Series books populated most of the shelves: *The Nature Library, Library of the Americas, The World Library,* and *The History of the United States*. About a dozen spiral-bound technical writing manuals occupied the far end of the lowest shelf. I suppose he had them for his work as an engineer, but I never saw him open a book, none of them—not once.

*Why do you have so many books if you don't read them?*

Dad built a long dining room table, and Mom found swing-back chairs that pinched my fingers more than once. A sideboard to store the "good china and crystal" and a hi-fi with shelves to hold records completed the room. On Saturday afternoons, Dad sometimes stacked three LPs on the hi-fi changer, and music filled the house for hours: Stravinsky, Rimsky-Korsakov, Harry Belafonte, Lena Horne. Broadway show tunes from the musicals we had seen together: *The Sound of Music, My Fair Lady, Gigi, The King and I*. From time to time, he slipped on some Latin music, held me in his arms with my feet on top of his, and taught me to dance: Cha-cha, Samba, Mambo.

Mom and Dad turned one of the bedrooms into a den. We called it the brown room because of the wood paneling Dad installed halfway up the walls. Above it, Mom pasted dull and unattractive wallpaper—beige with geometric flowers of ochre, dull brown, muted orange, and avocado green.

In keeping with the color scheme, the furniture, too, was brown—a corner table, couches, and rug.

Once in a while, we ate our TV dinners there instead of at the kitchen table. Chet Huntley and David Brinkley served up the evening news. We digested popular shows—*Ozzie and Harriet*, *My Three Sons*, and *Father Knows Best*—programs that, in retrospect, seem like brainwashing: designed to reinforce the benefits of the post-war culture shift. Men were the sole breadwinners who smoked like chimneys and enjoyed two martini lunches. Wives were domesticated homemakers who cleaned their houses in shirtwaist dresses, obsessed over the children, and served dinner at six on the dot. Every episode left me with the uneasy awareness that my home was quite different from the ones on TV. I never witnessed tenderness or adoration between my parents like Ozzie and Harriet had for one another, not a kiss or hug. And while Mom was deferential to Dad, I did not have the confidence the TV children did: that father knew best. Unlike Ozzie, Dad was unpredictable—home some nights and not others. In contrast to the upbeat Jim Anderson in *Father Knows Best*, my dad was inconsistent—happy one minute, mean the next. I was not over five years old, but I was old enough to sense there was something out of the ordinary.

My baby blue bedroom shared a wall with the brown room. Mom furnished it with a French provincial bed and dresser—her choice, not mine. "It's fit for a princess," she pled in response to my turned-up nose. I did not want to be squeezed into her mold. I preferred to play with boys, climb trees, and dig in the dirt, a reality that earned me her scorn.

Dad built shelves under the windows to hold my toys. The first occupants were Tiny Tears and Chatty Cathy. Over time, I populated the shelves with a pink plastic 45 RPM record player and records, a few Nancy Drew books, a faux Barbie doll (for some reason long forgotten, I was not allowed to have a real one), and a goldfish bowl. The goldfish bowl had a lifespan of three goldfish. One by one, they jumped to their death onto my white rug. After the third suicide, the waterless bowl with blue rocks in the bottom sat on the lower shelf and haunted me with its search for a reason for being.

*Why have a goldfish bowl if you have no goldfish?*

There was a strangeness to Mom and Dad's room. It was not the curtains with the black and mustard yellow Picasso-style print—they were just plain ugly. It was not the two twin beds separated by a single nightstand. I thought it suited them if it was good enough for Lucy and Ricky Ricardo. But it stirred enough curiosity in me to ask Mom about it one day. I sat at the kitchen table doing homework while she chopped vegetables for her beef soup.

"Mom, my friend's parents have big beds. Why don't you and Dad have one?"

She put the knife down and turned around, so her hands were free for demonstration. "Your father doesn't roll over. He rises, flips mid-air, and crashes down on the mattress. No one can sleep through that."

I watched as her hands illustrated Dad's process. "Huh," I muttered and returned to my math problems without further conversation.

What made their room odd was the gallery of more than a dozen unframed, eight-by-ten-inch black-and-white photographs. Each one was mounted on a foam board and glued to the wall. I was the lone subject in all of them. An awkward-looking kid with a pixie haircut and teeth too big for my face. Dressed in blue pedal-pushers and a sleeveless tee shirt. In one, I stood beside my bike in the driveway. In another, I held a hula hoop. My nose was stuck in a flower in front of the house in still another. When I stood before the photos, I felt extraordinary and self-conscious at the same time. On display and vulnerable all at once.

*Why? Why am I plastered on this wall?*

Like most cellars, our basement was dark and eerie, lit by a few naked light bulbs that flickered when you pulled the cord to turn them on or off. I was certain it held a murky secret, a creepy mystery. When it came on, the furnace roared and shook. The sump pump in the corner clicked and rattled before it began its rhythmic clunk-clunk-clunk. All the racket sent shivers down my spine. I refused to go there unless Mom or Dad went with me.

Dad's workshop filled the back corner, where he mounted pegboards on the walls and filled them with every tool imaginable. His workbench was piled high with cigar boxes filled with screws, washers, nuts, and bolts. He had all he could possibly need for the next project. Marble-topped end tables for the living room. Outdoor Christmas decorations. A doghouse. The floor was always coated with a layer of sawdust. My hunger for his attention posed as an offer to help.

"What can I do, Daddy? Can I help?"

"Yes. You can watch."

"That's not helping."

"Fine. Hold this real still while I drill a hole." He placed my hand out of harm's way, and I held fast to the wood. But when the wood began to shake, my young muscles were no match for the vibration. The wood slipped.

"I told you to hold it still!" he blasted. I ran off, my heart sinking into my shoes as I leapt up the stairs.

*Why do you have a child you don't to want bother with?*

He turned to his easel and oil paints if he had no house project to complete. Enamored with the work of the Dutch painter Piet Mondrian, he covered canvases with blocks of primary colors, blue, red, and yellow, with black lines to separate them. He moved on to emulate Van Gogh, to replicate still life, *Blue Enamel Coffeepot, Earthenware, and Fruit.* And because Dad's middle name was Vincent, he signed every painting in the bottom right corner "Vincent."

Dad fashioned one portion of the basement into a French-themed rec room. He painted the cinder block walls pink, and glued thick dark green felt carpet to the concrete floor. He dropped ceiling tiles to conceal the beams and ductwork. Mom furnished it with a gray couch soft enough to swallow me whole, a round glass-topped table, and four pink chairs to give the room ambiance and a sense of intimacy. After all that work, the room was seldom used.

*Why do you spend so much energy on this space that sits empty?*

Mom had her hobbies downstairs, too: old, cracked, and splintered antiques needing repair, bottles of homemade wine, and boxes filled with tear-off pads of children's stationery. She tinkered and toyed with stuff, but it was rare for her to pursue a project to completion.

There were shelves for storage and a chest freezer filled with a side of Black Angus beef. In the fall of 1962, I came home from school after an air raid drill, terrified by what the exercise meant. Mom assured me we would be safe down there with plenty of food. Still, her words were not enough to keep at bay my nightmares of soldiers in gas masks charging down the stairs, rifles in hand, to take us hostage. I was nine years old during the Cuban missile crisis, and alarm about a possible attack on our shores spread nationwide, but there was already an inner assault eating away at my soul.

# CHAPTER 3

"What is your earliest memory?" My therapist went straight to the heart of the matter at the beginning of my second session. She was not messing around. I had not even situated myself on the blue couch. I wrinkled my nose and looked for the tissues.

*I don't want to do this. But if I don't, I will never heal.*

Without lifting my chin, I focused on the white ceiling where it met the wall. I took a deep breath and closed my eyes.

I was three years old. Warm sunshine coaxed us to the front yard. Dad held me in his arms as we stood on the sidewalk with Mom and houseguests who had been visiting. They admired the brilliant colors of the flower garden that framed the walk and stretched across the front yard. White and blue pansies. Purple irises. We were all dressed in our Sunday best, and everyone seemed happy. Then, without warning, I found myself slipping from Dad's arms. My yellow dress was sliding. I was sinking. The concrete below looked hard, and I was sure if I tumbled down, it would hurt unless I spoke up.

"Hold me right, Daddy," I trembled. But as he hiked me up on his hip, he laughed. Our guests followed suit. Their belly laughter clawed at me. Embarrassment oozed from the scratches leaving me humiliated. My heart plummeted though my body did not. I folded in on myself like a wilted iris in Mom's garden.

"What do you wish had happened that day?" Sarah wondered.

"I wanted Mom to take me from Dad's arms. I wanted her to take me inside and comfort me, to rescue me from my shame. I wanted to be taken seriously."

That did not happen. Mom did not extract me from the scene. Instead, I melted. Mortified for stating my need. It was clear: I was responsible for my own safety. No one else would save me. So, I dug a hole in the silty gray sand and crawled in. Like a hermit crab, I pulled the grit over myself. Afraid of being mocked, I shut down. If I needed attention, I dared to emerge from my hole. And when I did, I did not cower. I demanded. The screaming in my head turned outward. It was the only way I knew to be seen or heard.

Caved in on myself, I was safe in my room. I created a world of imaginary friends and gave "real" identities to my dolls, who were my faithful companions. In my bedroom, I curled up like a roly-poly bug. But I was unaware that, even in my self-constructed safe space, my body, mind, and spirit absorbed the toxicity that swirled around me. My body was numb. My mind walled itself into compartments to store particular memories. My heart was robbed of curiosity and joy. In the privacy of my room, I reminded myself every day that no one cared for me, no one loved me. In public, I functioned as an average child and assumed the behavior of the consummate "good girl" to stay out of trouble.

*Do what you are told. Do not bother with questions. Always smile. Be polite.*

Sure, I bit my cousin once. She took the building blocks I was playing with. I could not let her get away with that. No one else would help me. What choice did I have?

Beyond that, I worked hard not to betray my inner turmoil. Grownups whispered when they thought I could not hear. Friends of my parents looked at me as through rose-colored glasses. "She's adorable," they murmured.

Relatives looked at me through a magnifying glass to rationalize my behavior. "She's tired. Or hungry. It's her Latin genes."

Gram's lens was the least forgiving. "She's spoiled."

The range of remarks confused me, but especially that one. She consistently chose the biggest piece of chicken and put it on my plate, bought me the dress with the most ruffles, or disallowed me from putting my hands in hot dish water. If that wasn't spoiling, I don't know what was. Still, her words were superglue, sticking relentlessly to my ego. I absorbed her critique as though it was my own, as if I could fix it. I was spoon-fed what I did not want, but it was not my fault. I never aspired to be a princess.

*Was that Mom's strategy? If she treated me like a princess, would I behave like one?*

I was too young to let the comments fall away. Instead, I internalized them. I took each one to heart as my hunger to be wanted and loved deepened to no avail. Before I turned four, I was persuaded that I was the problem. Looking back, it all seems so insignificant, so unimportant. And yet, these were the markers that left deep, unforgettable scars on my psyche. There had to be something more.

# CHAPTER 4

Gram and Gramps lived just thirty minutes away from us, in the house where they had raised their two children. Soon after my third birthday, they sold that home and moved to a twenty-five-acre farm on the Eastern Shore of Virginia, five hours away.

Gram had dreamed of moving to the Shore since her freshman year in college when she visited Davis Wharf for Thanksgiving weekend with her roommate, Edna. I imagine a younger Emily traveling from Lynchburg to Norfolk by train. There, they boarded the ferry to cross the Chesapeake Bay to Cape Charles, the southernmost point on the Shore. The wind blew through her chestnut brown hair as she leaned over the boat's railing. Her eyelids pinched out the intense sunshine as her gray-blue eyes followed the fishing boats that bobbed in the swells. A broad smile etched her face when she filled her lungs with the brisk, salty air of the Bay. Her laughter rang out as the seagulls swooped across the boat's bow. Emily found a deep, spiritual connection to the land and the water around it. The magic there so captivated her that she chose the Shore as her destiny and resolved to retire there one day.

Eight years after that first visit to the Shore, as the world emerged from the Spanish flu, she and Herman were married on Christmas Eve in a quiet church wedding. Herman vowed to love, honor, and cherish her while also making the unspoken promise to retire to the Shore together when the time came. They visited often over the years as their children grew, and when Gramps hung up his chemical engineer's apron for the last time, he was ready to transition to the peace of the Shore.

The plain, two-story, two-bedroom white clapboard house with three barns sat on the banks of Nandua Creek, with a small, protected cove to the left of the property. Because the cost of the farm was a stretch for their bank account, Mary, Herman's sister, moved in with them and paid monthly rent. Gram would have preferred not to have Mary with them, but she tolerated her presence as a means to an end. Gramps rented out three of the twenty-five acres to be cultivated as a pine forest; when mature, the trees would be cut and sold for lumber. He was determined to make ends meet.

Forty-four years after the onset of Gram's love affair with the Shore, on another Thanksgiving weekend, Mom, Dad, and I traveled to the farm. It was my first real road trip, and I watched the flurry of activity around me as the preparations were made. Mom packed sandwiches and drinks in the red, black, and beige Skotch cooler. She placed a bag filled with dolls, crayons, and coloring books in the backseat of our blue Ford station wagon. Dad checked the tires, the windshield wipers, and the oil. When all the items on the list had been checked off, we drove "over the river and through the woods to grandmother's house," as the song goes. I was a restless young traveler who whined before we started down the Garden State Parkway.

"How much longer?"

"Why don't you lay down and take a little nap?" Mom suggested.

I put my head on the cold vinyl seat and closed my eyes. A cool breeze came through Dad's window and blew on my face. I heard Mom shuffle through radio stations in search of some music to quiet me. Sleep found me and drifted me away for a couple of hours. When I woke, I pulled the coloring book and crayons from the bag and scribbled my way through the pages until the car eased off the highway and into a service station. I sat up.

"Where are we?"

"We are stopping for gas. Let's take a potty break," Mom said.

I climbed from the car, stretched my arms out, and took a deep breath. The air smelled salty.

"How much longer, Mom? I'm hungry."

"We will eat our sandwiches when we get back in the car."

With the pitstop complete, we were back on the road. No sooner had I settled in than I peered out the window and noticed we were eye to eye with a flock of birds. Awe overshadowed my hunger.

"Mom! Where are we?"

"We are on a tall bridge."

"Why are the birds so close?" I squealed as I pointed out the window.

The white gulls with black faces weaved around us. When I looked beyond them to the water, my stomach fell. The water below was too far away.

"Mom, what are those white dots down there? And why is all that snow behind them?"

"Oh. Those are motorboats, and the white streams behind them are the waves made by the boat motors."

The end of the bridge was in sight. The houses and docks on the shore grew larger. I sighed in relief when the bridge returned us to solid ground. Then I remembered I was hungry. "I'm hungry."

Mom reached into the cooler at her feet and pulled out a sandwich wrapped in wax paper. She pulled away the paper, put a napkin around it, and reached over the seat to hand it to me. I took a bite and savored the peanut butter and jelly. It might have been the best sandwich I had ever had; it tasted so good.

"I need some milk," I mumbled with the sticky peanut butter in my mouth.

Mom unscrewed the cap from the gray thermos and poured the milk until the cup was half full. "Be careful," she warned as she handed it to me.

My stomach was full, so I turned to my dolls to "feed them lunch." By the time they "finished eating," I was ready for another nap. I put my head back down, put my arm around my "babies," and dozed off. When I woke up the second time, I sat up to see flatlands and sandy brown fields framed by tall pine forests. We passed one fenced pasture with horses and another with cows. The car meandered through villages with weathered storefronts and tiny white houses with blue shutters. Everything was more spread out here than at home. The few people I saw sat in chairs on their porches. I wondered where all the rest of the people were.

Over time, I learned the Eastern Shore is a peninsula on the east side of the Bay, detached from the mainland of Virginia. A phantom limb from the rest of the body of the Old Dominion. Where watermen have made their living for centuries by fishing, crabbing, and mucking oysters and clams. Where farmers have planted and harvested corn, tobacco, tomatoes, melons, and soybeans for generations. Even with the Tyson and Perdue chicken farms and factories that now provide jobs to migrant workers, the Shore is sprawling farmland that time forgot.

At last, we turned off the highway and onto a narrow country road. The distances between houses grew wider and wider, with endless fields between them until, at last, the car slowed to a crawl.

"This is our turn," Mom said to Dad as she pointed at the road sign.

The county lane was flanked by tall pine trees that cast one long, dark shadow across our path. I was not sure whether I felt hugged and safe or intimidated and tentative. All I knew was we would soon be at Gram and Gramps' house, which was good because I needed to pee—very badly. As we approached the long, sandy drive, Dad slowed the car to a snail's pace. A small, hand-painted sign leaning against a fencepost greeted us with a cautionary message: "10 MPH." Beyond the sign was a rusted, barbed-wire fence laced with orange-flowered trumpet vines. To the right of the lane was a wide-open field. We rounded a bend, and there it was—an unremarkable white house in the middle of a field of unmown grass. Dad inched the car up to the front porch where Gram and Gramps stood with grins on their faces so wide their cheeks disappeared.

"You made it!" Gram was giddy as we unfolded and pulled ourselves from the car. "Come in. Have a drink. I made brownies!"

Mom hugged her parents as she rushed past them and pushed me in the front door. "Where's the bathroom?" Gramps pointed to the door inside.

When we returned to the yard, Gram and Gramps were talking with Dad about the farm, the cove, and another farm across the water. Gram was heavyset, with her white hair pulled into a bun on the back of her head. She wore a light blue dress and a sweater. In his gray slacks, plaid shirt, and beige sweater vest, Gramps clacked his false teeth as I ran toward him. He scooped me up and hugged me tight. For a second, I felt complete, happy, welcome. But in an instant, my senses kicked in.

"What stinks? It smells like rotten eggs."

Gramps picked me up and walked toward the cove, where the tall grass gave way to taller, darker, thicker grass. "This is marsh grass," he said as he pointed to what lay before us. "Do you see the mud out there?"

I nodded.

"That dark brown mud is what you smell. The water will rise and cover it all up in a little while, and it won't smell so bad."

"Promise?"

He snickered. "Of course."

"Put me down, Gramps."

He lowered me to the ground, took my hand, and we waded through the high weeds back towards the house. To Gramps' surprise, I stopped and crouched in the grass taller than I was. I had an idea.

"I'll hide here, Gramps. You come find me!"

We played my version of hide and seek until I wore out.

"I'm thirsty. Do you think we can go eat brownies now?"

"You betcha!" Gramps snickered.

We walked in the front door where the aroma of fresh brownies still hung in the air. The house was modest, but to me, it may as well have been a mansion surrounded by wide open acres. Large couches sat on either end of the living room with a fireplace on the side wall between them. An upright piano, a bookcase, and three easy chairs filled out the gigantic room. Enormous sliding glass windows provided gorgeous views of the water from every room. No matter the weather, those views invited themselves into the house all day, every day. There was no hiding from the beauty of the farm.

The dining room flowed into the kitchen on the other side of the house. There were two bedroom suites upstairs, one on either side of the staircase. Aunt Mary's blue room and bath were on the left. She had furnished it with a full bed, two dressers, and a big round table that was always covered with letters and pictures her friends had sent her, with her own cards and envelopes to be sent in return. Gram and Gramps used the pink room and bath on the other side of the landing. In addition to a bed and two dressers, Gram had a sewing machine in one corner next to her rocking chair. In the opposite corner was a small twin bed: my bed. Knowing that they cared enough to dedicate a small bed to me was all the comfort I needed.

After a good look upstairs, we returned to the dining room and sat at the large round table in its big leather chairs. I savored the warm blonde brownie and washed it down with a small glass of milk that was so cold it made my head hurt. I was eager to get back outdoors before it got dark. "Gramps, let's go back outside. I want to see what else is here!"

We walked out the front door, down three steps, and headed toward the cove, stopping at a door at the end of the house.

"Here's the pump house," Gramps explained. He tugged at the door, which opened to a greasy black furnace and a well pump. We moved inside into a small room Gramps had fashioned into a darkroom. Black curtains were pulled back from the windows to shed light on the camera equipment, bottles filled with solutions, and a small sink.

We stepped back into the cool air and walked over to the three white barns with red roofs that flanked the property's west side. Each barn served a different purpose. Barn one was home to the black Chrysler and Gramp's workshop. A long wooden counter held chemical-filled bottles lined up in a row like army soldiers in brown uniforms. The potbelly stove in the middle of the floor warmed the garage in the winter, but the smell of smoke stayed year-round. The middle barn was home to the red Farmall tractor and the small fishing boat Gramps bought soon after they purchased the farm. Gram placed a refrigerator freezer along the back wall. Because they had survived the depression, she took what precautions she could to ensure they and their houseguests never went hungry. The third barn, with three doors leading to smaller chambers, was home to a hodgepodge of stuff. Behind door number one were brown wooden trunks, one of which was filled with Gramps' coveted and extensive stamp collection. Rickety chairs and tables without legs, a cabinet with glass doors hanging from half of a hinge, stacks of chipped plates, cups, and saucers, and pocked aluminum pots filled the second room. In the third chamber, Gram stored her gardening tools and flowerpots, and Gramps stacked fishing supplies: rods, reels, nets, and tackle boxes.

The last place still to be explored was at the far end of the lawn. Gramps took my hand, and we headed toward the dock. The tall grass whipped against my legs and tickled my face, but instead of bothering me, it added to my sense of freedom and safety. Until we got to the dock. The planks were narrow, and the water was there—right under my feet. I could not see the bottom of the creek and did not know how to swim. I hesitated.

*What if I slip?*

Gramps coached me as I cautiously put one foot in front of the other. "Take your time," he said and took my hand.

Gram relished every minute of life on the Shore. This was her heaven on earth. I was too young to grasp the depth of her love for this place, but I experienced a sense of paradise even on this first visit. It was perfect—all of it. Beautiful. Safe. I had no concern for monsters under my bed. No loud trucks rumbling down the street. No fears of soldiers kidnapping me. Instead, dogs bayed in the distance and shattered the quiet of the evening. An orange and pink sunset spanned the sky until the crescent moon rose like a puppet pulled up by strings from the heavens. There were no city lights to dilute the brilliance of the night sky, so I watched the dark dome fill with sparkling white dots on an ink-black canvas. Once in a while, one of the dots streaked across the deep night in a quest to catch the sun. As the early morning light peeked over the farmland, a small boat puttered on the Creek. It motored its way to the headwaters while seagulls swept close behind, a screeching choir of beggars demanding their breakfast be tossed overboard.

    The Shore quickly became as magical for me as it was for Gram. It was holy ground. Nature was there to snatch me up and hold me as tight as Gramps had. God's world embraced me. And I grew to love all of it. Even the stinky low tide. It settled in my core and became my home away from home. Beyond the farm, all of the Shore captured me with its simplicity and slower pace of life. It teemed with goodness and grace. This world seemed quiet and uncomplicated. Spending time there was akin to having your car windshield wiped clean: only clear glass between you and what life was intended to be.

# CHAPTER 5

The farm, my home away from home, offered me the serenity and safety of an easy chair and a warm cup of tea. My proper home was like a hot potato burning my hands if I held it for more than half a second. Intuitively, I knew there was a stark contrast between my two worlds. Insecurity had squirmed its way into my psyche long before I could articulate it. It drove my life at home but not at the farm.

What gave birth to such fragility? Was it the scary basement? The bully-children at nursery school? The train that blared its horn on its way through town? When did I become so afraid of the world around me? Where did it begin? All I knew was that it burrowed into all of me bit by bit.

My Dad's mom, mi abuela, lived in Spanish Harlem in New York City. Visits to her accentuated my fears. My body shuddered as Dad drove us up the Turnpike when the planes approaching Newark airport looked like they might graze the top of the car.

*If the plane hits the car, we will be crushed.*

My stomach churned when we entered the grimy, diesel-fumed tunnel under the Hudson River. I held my breath as I imagined the walls breaking and water rushing in to swallow us whole.

*If the walls crumble, we will die.*

My trepidation did not stop when Dad parked the car. The dangers seemed to close in on me as we wound through the streets. We dodged angry-looking men carrying briefcases, side-stepped yippy dogs on leashes, and swerved around stinky trash bags. I kept my head down and my eyes focused on my feet.

*Don't step on a subway grate—you might fall in.*
*Don't step in the dog poop—you'll ruin your black patent leather shoes.*
*Don't step in a gutter puddle—you'll soil your white lace socks.*

This was no farm. Tall buildings instead of rolling fields. Congested streets instead of country lanes. Angry faces. Loud noises. Repulsive smells—worse than the mud of the Creek. Even the sapling planted in a small patch of soil on the sidewalk struggled to survive. Concrete stood in for nature here.

The scores of different sights, sounds, and smells assaulted my senses. Laundry hung on balcony clotheslines above the boys who played dodgeball in the courtyard below. Women gossiped across the chasm between the buildings while men in sleeveless t-shirts yelled obscenities in Spanish at their sons playing ball. Latin music bounced off the buildings while the aroma of black beans and carne asada drifted from the tenement windows.

We climbed the four flights of dark, dingy stairs to mi abuela's one-bedroom, sparsely furnished apartment. A crucifix hung on a pale pink wall in her sitting room. A pillar candle with a picture of the Virgin Mary backlit by the flame inside sat on a cream-colored doily on the small rickety table below. Rosary beads, a tiny white Bible, and a milk-white vase with a fake rosebud posed next to the candle. I noticed the difference between her cross and mine—hers, with a crucified Jesus, scared the daylights out of me.

Mi abuela was a short, round woman with a flat nose and huge breasts. Her graying black hair was pulled away from her face and sat atop her head, held by a brown carved Spanish comb. She cooked a delicious meal of hallacas—Venezuelan tamales with pork, beef, chicken, onions, and olives. The aroma drew me into her kitchen, but I could never get enough of her dessert, bienmesabe—rum-soaked lady fingers topped with coconut cream.

She always seemed sad to me, but I did not know why. I imagined she was lonely, but the creases in her forehead spoke of worry. I was too young to know her story, and she spoke too little English to tell me. There was no way for me to access what might bother her, but I would learn in time.

🌰

Mom and Dad entered me in my first baby parade when I was four years old. They had been to one before we moved from the river house and were eager to get me on a float when I was old enough. I was dressed like Chiquita Banana in a tiny multi-colored bikini that mi abuela had sewn at Dad's request. A crown of bananas heavier than my head completed the ensemble. Mom perched me on a small platform and surrounded me with more fruit—bananas, pineapples, and mangoes. She pulled me down the parade route while Dad took pictures from the sidewalk. They beamed with pride when I was awarded the first-place trophy.

The following year, my float was larger, with a platform painted green to suggest a grassy pasture. I sat on a small, three-legged stool in a pink pinafore dress, holding a shepherd's crook. A little lamb tethered to the float trembled beside me. It bleated for mercy, begging to be set free. Mom and Dad wanted more than a third-place finish, but I was not bothered at all. What disturbed me was what happened days later when Mom served up lamb chops and vegetables for supper.

I looked up from my plate at Mom in the middle of dinner. It dawned on me that I had not seen the lamb, which had been living in the garage, that afternoon. "Where's my lamb?"

Their mouths gaped. They stared at me for a long second before looking down at their plates to push around their peas and carrots. They never answered my question.

Dad traveled for business and was home for dinner two or three times a week. On those nights, Mom served a home-cooked meal instead of TV dinners, fish sticks, or frozen pot pies. She put on her orange apron with white rick-rack piping and prepared a delicious dinner from scratch: coq au vin or chicken divan, beef stew, or spaghetti with meatballs. The house smelled better than Snuffy's, our favorite restaurant. But her efforts seemed to go unnoticed and were often overshadowed in an instant by Dad's troubles.

"Say grace," he bellowed at me.

I did as I was told, but my voice wobbled, and he became impatient. "Dios mio! Amen!"

The food smelled so good, and I piled more on my plate than I could ever eat. "I'm full. I can't eat anymore."

His anger flared. "Children are starving in China. Finish your dinner. Clean your plate!"

*Why don't you send the leftovers to China?*

Shame rushed over me like water crashing over a seawall. I did not know who, what, or where China was, and I did not care to know. Instead, I melted into a puddle of tears and prepared to drown in it. Mom sat silent.

Another night, I spilled a glass of milk. It streamed across the table and dribbled down onto the floor. Dad slammed his fork down on his plate and started to yell at me. I withered inside. Mom jumped up from the table and screamed, "Get in the car and lock the doors!"

Terror enveloped me. My skin was on fire. I ran down the steps, into the garage, and jumped into the bucket seat of Mom's gray Karmann Ghia.

*If I lock the doors, Mom won't be able to get in the car. What will happen then?*

I decided not to lock the doors and waited, but quaked like a leaf on a tree while I dared to imagine what was happening inside.

*Was Dad hitting her? Did he take a knife from the drawer? Is she going to die?*

I tried to nurse my hysteria and held my breath between sobs.

*She will come out and get in the car. She will be OK. I will be OK. We will be OK.*

I caught my breath when she finally ran into the garage. She jumped in the car. She put the key in the ignition, started the engine, and pushed the stick shift into reverse. When she turned to guide the car down the driveway, she noticed my door was not locked.

"I told you to lock the doors! Why didn't you do as I told you?"

"I was afraid you wouldn't be able to get in," my voice shook. A lamb led to slaughter. I wept and shuddered, uncertain about whose wrath scared me more. My concern for her safety was also for my own, but she did not see it my way.

*I cannot get anything right. Someone is always mad at me or yelling at me.*

I do not recall where we went that night or when we went home. Life went on as though nothing had happened. Dad's anger and verbal abuse frightened me enough, but his unpredictability shook the ground under my feet. When he was home, I was never sure which Dad was there. Nice Daddy? Angry Daddy? Sober Daddy? Drunk Daddy? No one knew. No one dared anticipate. The worst of it was I never felt safe.

There was a small recess in the corner of our garage where Mom had placed a cabinet to store her garden supplies. My pink bike with training wheels, a bell, a white and pink plastic-weave basket, and tassels was parked beside it. One day, Mom took me to the garage and stood me in front of the tall, canary-yellow metal cabinet. It loomed over me like a ghost in a haunted house. The nasty smell of fertilizer made me gag.

"Do not ever open this cabinet. Do not touch it. It is full of poisons that will kill you."

Her words paralyzed me. How could I extract my bike from the space between the cabinet and the wall?

*Can I back it out with one hand while holding my nose with the other? Will one wrong move make it wobble and topple and send the contents flying and killing me in an instant?*

My discomfort in the world was growing inside of me and taking on a life of its own. I sensed Mom wanted to protect me, but her messages were filled with her own dread. By my fifth birthday, I was hungrier for attention than protection. I must have believed that if I could get them to pay attention to me, whatever the cost, I would be safe.

On Valentine's Day, I carried a shoe box filled with Valentine's cards and candy from school. The school bus stopped at the corner, and the driver opened the door while the neighborhood kids pushed and shoved one another in the aisle to get off. I waited for the aisle to clear and clutched my box close to my chest. When everyone else was off, I ran to the steps; my foot slipped, my skirt blew up, and I tumbled to the street. The lid flew off the shoebox, and cards and candy sprawled on the pavement all around me. The bus driver closed the door and drove off. All the other children were gone. No one was there to help me. No one to collect the cards and candy. No one to see if I was hurt. Loneliness burned deeper than the scrapes on my knees.

One week later, I went home after an afternoon of sledding with the neighborhood kids. Climbing the front steps, I noticed the green plants in the garden by the porch. The one covered in soft brown fur prompted my curiosity, and I bent over to pick it up. When I tried pulling the mitten off my left hand, I realized the cactus spines had burrowed through the mittens and into my fingertips. I ran into the house, wailing, looking for Mom.

"What have you done?" She huffed.

"I didn't know," I winced, alarmed by her disgust.

"Sit down. I need to get tweezers and a magnifier."

She sat next to me and extracted the spines from my hands one by one. Her jaws were clamped. Her eyes were narrowed and her brow furrowed. She was more than aggravated—she was red hot with anger.

"You won't be going to the circus."

It crushed me to miss the circus, but harder to stomach was the overwhelming and superseding silence that filled the room for the hour it took to get off my mittens.

*What will it take to feel loved in this house?*

A growing sense of isolation exacerbated my need to feel loved. I acted out in hopes of someone paying attention. I fell into the next-door neighbor's koi pond. I stepped in every pile of dog poo or piece of chewing gum in my path. I went out the backdoor to get the milk from the milk box on a chilly day and slipped on the icy slate. When I tried to catch myself, the bottle slipped from my hand, the milk spewed, shattered glass sliced my leg, and a river of pink milk trickled into the grass. Mom was more upset about the wasted milk than my injury. She was often exasperated with me and unable to muster compassion most days.

*I am an inconvenience.*

Later that fall, in the Emergency Room at Mountainside Hospital, the doctor inquired of Mom, "What was she doing that could have provoked such a severe asthma attack?"

"She was running around like a wild Indian."

"Well, she has pneumonia. I'm admitting her to the children's ward for treatment."

They placed me in an oxygen tent to assist my breathing and under an apron of ice to reduce my temperature. I had Mom and Dad's attention. After two weeks, they took me home wrapped in a bubble of protection. Mom drove me to Kenilworth every week for allergy shots. My activities at home and at school were restricted, if not prohibited.

"Why can't I play in the leaves?"

"The mold will make you sick."

"Why can't I have Coke or chocolate cake?"

"They will make you sick."

"Why can't we have a live Christmas tree?"

"A real tree will make you sick. We will get a lovely white plastic one and decorate it with gumballs and used flashbulbs covered with glitter."

I was disappointed, and my disappointment turned to anger. My anger turned to loneliness, and loneliness melted my heart like a candle.

My friend, Sheryl, lived down the street. Her mom was going to have a baby. Jackie, my mom's friend, was pregnant too.

*I need a little brother or sister.*

I was tired of feeling so alone. My friends with sisters shared their bedrooms, their toys, their clothes. I wanted a live-in playmate too. But more than that, I wanted someone to share the experience of what it was like to live with my parents, to be in this family. I needed someone who, like me, was verbally assaulted by one parent and neglected by the other.

I started to beg. "Mom! I want a baby brother. Or a sister. Either one."

My words must have evaporated before they reached her ears because she never responded. Over time, my whiny demand turned into a need for an explanation.

"Why can't I have a baby brother or sister?"

"I don't want any more children. They fight all the time. I don't want to spend my time breaking up your fights."

I internalized her answer and convinced myself I was less-than. Less than what she wanted. Less than what she wanted me to be. Did she even want me at all?

*I'm not good enough. I don't deserve a sibling. I need to do better, be better.*

Fear, rejection, and embarrassment eroded my character before my seventh birthday. They were the automatic drivers of my behavior, and my reactions became disproportionate to the threats. One afternoon, I went down the street to Sheryl's house to play. We played a game of Chutes and Ladders until another friend of hers arrived.

"Cathy doesn't want to play with you. You need to go home."

I turned away so Sheryl could not see my tears. She did not tell me twice. I ran down the stairs and out the door and jumped on my bike to ride home. Tears of rejection spurted from my eyes as I waited at the corner to watch for oncoming cars. A man drove up next to me and rolled down his window.

"Can I help you?"

I imagined him reaching out, grabbing me, and pulling me in. Mom's words echoed in my head, "Don't get in cars with strangers."

In panic, I took off as fast as I could.

A month later, I stood in my front yard as a couple of boys who lived around the corner charged toward me and threatened to pull my pants down. Their words violated me. My hysteria was visceral, but even at the time, it felt like an irrational, unexplained response. I wondered why my reaction was so severe.

# CHAPTER 6

By the time I turned seven, I was so turned in on myself I had little understanding of how the unhealthy environment in my home impacted me. Instead of shaking off feelings of blame or shame, I dug my hole deeper. Instead of speaking up for myself, I recoiled, certain that I was damaged.

Mom drove me to Orange, a nearby town, one afternoon to take a battery of tests. She would not tell me what the tests were for. My imagination took over and fed my suspicions about my impairments.

*They are going to know I am dumb. What will they do with me?*

I wanted to believe the tests were related to school, but Mom would not discuss it. I sensed that they were sheltering me from some truth, but I did not know what it was. The final exercise required me to position a group of blocks to match the picture on the paper on the desk before me. As I pushed the rearranged blocks over to the tester, I saw I had made a mistake. But it was too late. I was too intimidated to take it back. I was too scared to try to fix it. I went home feeling stupid.

My self-esteem sank by the day. If my parents noticed, they either did not know what to do or did not care. They were wrapped in their own drama. Dad drank more, and the more he drank, the more Mom withdrew. When he poured his cocktail, I looked at Mom and saw a turtle pulling her head into her shell.

I noticed her deference to Dad for the first time the evening after my friend, Betsy, had been playing with me at the house. We kicked a ball around the backyard until I suggested we go inside and play a board game. Betsy did not want to go inside, so she stomped off. I went to my room and played alone. Minutes later, I heard the phone ring. After Mom said, "Hello," there was silence. Then, "Okay. Thank you for letting me know."

"BJ, come here," she hollered.

I could not believe she called me that, but I stepped into the kitchen across the hall from my room.

Mom was rolling meatballs. "Betsy's mother called."

"Am I in trouble?"

"Wait until your father gets home," she replied, her eyes focused on her hands as she mashed and molded the greasy meat between her palms.

Dad was already angry when he walked in the door that evening. He tossed his briefcase on the dining room table and went straight to the whiskey. Mom immediately told him her side of the story. I was given no chance to defend myself.

"Solitary confinement for two weeks!" he boomed.

"Two weeks?"

"You go to school. You come home. Nothing else."

*This is so unreasonable. And you didn't even hear my side of the story.*

Mom's lips were pursed as Dad took a dark red crayon and marked my punishment on the calendar. SOLITARY CONFINEMENT on every day to the end of the month. The next day, he left town on a business trip, and Mom was left to enforce my sentence. She let me know in her clipped words and body language that she, too, had been grounded. My innocent infraction interfered with her bridge schedule, College Club meetings, and Children's Playhouse rehearsals. A cold silence filled the house for the next two weeks.

I was a week out of solitary before I contracted scarlet fever and missed ten days of school. While I was home, my teacher had the class make get-well cards for me. Most of them were kind in a predictable way.

"I miss you in class."

"I hope you feel better soon."

"Get well."

But one was different.

"I hate you, and I hope you never come back to school." It was from Betsy.

Mom wondered why the teacher had not pulled that one card from the pile. Dad got angry and stormed around the house. But they took no action, and they never spoke to me about it. I was confused by their double standard: it was okay for Betsy to be mean to me but not for me to stand up for what I wanted. When I returned to school, I was on my own to figure out how to relate to Betsy. We never played together again.

My circle of friends was shrinking, so Mom signed me up for after-school activities to keep me busy. She started with dance lessons. Every Wednesday afternoon, she drove me across town to the Knights of Columbus Hall, where she sat in a folding chair and watched a herd of little girls in black leotards as we pranced, hopped, skipped, and jumped across the wooden floor. Dance made me happy: my spirit found freedom in movement.

She signed me up for the children's theater production of *Ten Little Indians*. With my dark complexion and long straight brown hair, I fit the part of one little Indian. The cast learned its lines, but rehearsals were pandemonium with ten little children. Nevertheless, we practiced for our first performance at a rehabilitation center for children with severe health conditions. We were well prepared—well prepared for everything except the audience. The show was about to begin, so I ran down the hall to use the bathroom. I passed a child in an incubator whose appearance made my stomach flip over. Nausea overwhelmed me. I turned ghost-white, lost my focus and my lines, and refused to go on stage. The show went on fine with nine little Indians, but Dad, who had come for the performance, was unforgiving.

"What is wrong with you?" He ranted when we got in the car.

I knew no response would satisfy him, so I kept my mouth shut all the way home. That was the end of my acting career.

Mom signed me up for Brownies. I took the task of earning badges very seriously and was passionate in my pursuit of them. Each badge was a small victory for my bruised ego. I covered my sash with the sewing badge, cooking badge, knitting badge, and home health badge to start. I had my sights set on the camping badge, but to do so, I had to go to camp. So, when summer rolled around, I went to Camp Sinawik. Our leader sent the girls off on the first day to gather sticks for the bonfire. I stayed back because I wanted to help our counselors prepare lunch. And, if I was honest, I liked them better than my campmates. I wanted them to need, or at least want, my help. When I approached the counselor fixing lunch, she turned her nose up at me.

"What do you want?" she snarled.

"I thought I could help you here."

"No. I don't need your help. Go join the others." She snapped.

My insides collapsed. It was not her words that hurt the most. The way she said them made me want to slither on my belly into the woods. Tears welled up in my eyes and clouded my vision. I turned away from her and ran towards my campmates. But fifty feet away, I tripped over a massive tree root and put a huge gash in my left knee. The counselor heard the thud when I hit the ground, but she was busy peeling carrots and did not turn to see what happened. When she did see the dirt in the wound and the blood streaming down my leg, she rolled her eyes and let out an enormous, disgruntled sigh.

My face burned with embarrassment as my campmates gathered around and whispered to one another. Mom picked me up and took me home. I was too humiliated the next day and never returned to camp.

*So much for my camping badge.*

　　　　　　　　　　🌰

Mi abuela made a rare visit to our house for Easter dinner the following spring. She wore a beautiful purple dress with purple beads and a matching hat. I had never seen her look so fancy. She had been to Easter mass in the morning, and Dad picked her up from church and brought her straight to us. She shuffled in, sat on the living room couch, and called me over to her with a crooked index finger.

"When you come to see me the next time, I will take you to have your ears pierced."

Panic bolted down my spine like lightning. I had been getting allergy shots for months to control my asthma and had no interest in unnecessary needles. I spent the rest of her visit with my hands over my ears. That was the last time I saw her. Three weeks later, I came home from school to learn she had died.

"Your abuelita died. Your father is taking care of things."

Mom was matter-of-fact in her telling of it, as routine as washing the dishes or ironing the sheets. She did not embellish. She did not explain. She showed no emotion. There was no acknowledgment of grief. I did not know what to do with this, my first significant loss. So, I did nothing. I asked no questions. I shed no tears. I was too young to know what to say or do, and no one attempted to model for me how one could grieve. If there was a funeral or a wake, I was not included. I am not sure my mother was either.

*Mi abuela died. She is gone and she is not coming back.*

# CHAPTER 7

School recessed for the summer, so Mom, Dad, and I retreated to the Shore for a week. Gramps was happy to see us: he wanted our help putting the boat in the Creek. Boat days were the best days. If the sun was shining and it was not too hot, if the tide was high between ten in the morning and two in the afternoon, Gramps hooked the boat trailer to the tractor and backed the boat down the short concrete ramp into the Creek. Gram filled the Styrofoam cooler with sandwiches, fruit, and cold drinks and set it beside the green Evinrude motor in the stern. We stashed life preservers and fishing gear under the bow. Gramps sat at the wheel as we climbed down the steps to board the boat one at a time—first Gram, then Dad, then me. Mom stood on the dock to untie the ropes and push us off before she jumped in. Gramps backed the boat into the channel, and once we cleared the dock, he pointed us toward the Bay and revved the motor. I climbed onto the bow and grabbed hold of the rope, humming made-up tunes while the breeze blew back my hair and the sun warmed my face. I was as free as the seagulls who ushered us to the Bay. This was heaven.

The first day out, we passed neighboring farms and a well-weathered shack next to a towering pile of giant white clam shells. Then Gramps turned off the motor, and we pulled out our fishing rods and bait. Mom tossed the anchor overboard, and we lowered our lines into the water. We sat quietly and waited for the first nibbles on our lines as the boat bobbed from side to side with the incoming tide. All that disrupted the silence was the gentle lapping of the water against the boat and the gulls overhead clamoring for scraps of bait, until…

"Mom! Look! There's something tugging my line! What is it?" I had Christmas-morning-level excitement.

She reached over and helped me reel in my first catch: a light brown baby sand shark less than a foot long. It was too small to keep and unfit to eat, so Mom threw it back into the Creek. The sting of failure was real but momentary. Gramps offered comfort.

"There are a lot of fish in the sea, Janice."

He was right. There were trout, perch, spot, bluefish, and my favorite, blowfish (the non-poisonous variety)—when I scratched its belly, it puffed up and made me giggle. Whatever was edible, even the eels, went into the bucket and were taken home to be cleaned and cooked. Boat day always delivered.

If conditions were less than perfect to go out on the boat, Gram invited me to go with her to barn three. We pulled out the wheelbarrow and filled it with frozen chicken necks, crab lines, a net, and a bushel basket. We dropped everything on the dock, wrapped the bait with twine, threw the four lines into the water, and sat down for the long wait. Seagulls, ever hungry, gathered overhead and screeched for a handout. I yammered back at them, and Gram chuckled at me. It was oddly reassuring to hear her laugh—I felt seen.

At long last, a line wriggled, and we jumped into action. With care and precision, I pulled in the line while Gram set the net in the water. When I did my part as she instructed, she scooped the crab into the net and, with a canvas glove, dumped the crab into the basket, where the crusty green creature stared at us with beady gray eyes. It flailed its claws and hissed as if to scold us for its plight and threaten us with inevitable and painful revenge if we got close. A good day was a yield of a dozen blue crabs, which we took to the house for steaming and picking.

One afternoon, as Gram and I patiently waited for nibbles on our crab lines, she noticed the dock needed repair. Several gray two-by-four planks were dry-rotted. When she told Gramps of the danger, he and Dad made a trip to the lumber yard to purchase the necessary supplies. Back home, they went straight to work to replace the weathered wood. They started at the far end and worked their way toward the shoreline. About midway, Dad picked up a plank, turned around, and accidentally smacked Gramps in the back, sending him flying into the Creek. Gramps suffered a couple of cracked ribs and bruised legs, but he recovered in days. From my perspective, Dad did not. After the accident, he spent most of his time on the farm outdoors, alone. He walked along the marsh grass, smoked his Tiparillo cigarettes, and talked to himself. He created a small three-hole "golf course," bought a set of clubs, and wandered around the lawn, driving, slicing, shanking, and putting balls. After the dock accident, Dad traveled to the Shore with us less often.

"He has to travel for work," Mom rationalized. I was not sure it was true.

On a gray day, when the weather was too threatening to get in the boat, Gramps walked me to barn two, opened the door, and said, "Look. I found a little gift for you." He had bought a second-hand bike with a green frame. It leaned against the wall next to the tractor. I was ecstatic. Riding my bike was as liberating as sailing was. I guided the bike out to the grass. But the grass was too bumpy to navigate, so I pointed it down the sandy drive and rode down to the road and back as Gramps trotted close behind. When my legs gave out, he found the enormous orange basketball he had stored in barn three. He nailed a backboard on one of the locust trees and attempted to teach me how to shoot the ball. But it was bigger than my head and too heavy for my weak arms. When I started to whine, he cut me off.

"Come, follow me."

He walked to the pump house with me sprinting to keep up. Gramps closed the blackout curtains and showed me how he developed pictures. I was spellbound as I watched this magician at work. One by one, images appeared on paper—as if by magic out of thin air. Little by little, the gray blur took shape until I could make out the tree, the marsh grass, and the cove beyond. Gramps picked up the tongs, handed them to me, and showed me how to pull the paper from the solution and use clothespins to hang them on the line to dry.

I knew all about wooden clothespins. On laundry days, I helped Gramps pull long sticks from barn three and carry them to the clothesline strung between two trees. Gram brought out the freshly washed laundry, and together we clipped socks and shirts, underwear, and shorts to the line. When the lines were full and the hampers empty, Gramps handed me one of the sticks he had carved a notch in at the end, a notch big enough to fit the line in. He picked up the other stick, and I awaited his signal.

"One. Two. Three." Together, we pushed the line up and stood back to watch as the breeze billowed through the laundry.

On "garbage days," Gramps loaded the galvanized cans filled with food scraps and tins into the little blue trailer hitched to the back of the tractor. He lifted me onto the seat, and we rode down the lane to a small entry into the woods, where he stopped, jumped off, and emptied the cans into a pile of decomposed refuse. Compost before it was fashionable. I carried a bin of papers and walked with him to the makeshift incinerator of stacked concrete blocks. The paper in place, Gramps tossed in a match, and we stood side by side, watching the smoke unfurl and carry tiny sparks into the sky.

On Sundays, I rode with him to fetch the Baltimore Sun tucked into the plastic delivery tube at the end of the road. In the middle of the week, I sat in the front seat when he went to pick up Miss Hattie, the cleaning lady. I was Gramps' sidekick. He kept me busy and entertained. Time spent with him was pure joy.

In mid-July, Gramps pulled the black Chrysler to the front door. Gram climbed into the front seat, and Mom and I scooted into the back. We made the hour-long trek north to Chincoteague Island for the annual pony swim. People came from all over the peninsula to watch as the wild ponies were shepherded from Assateague Island across the channel to Chincoteague to be auctioned off. The pony swim lasted a matter of minutes, but a carnival atmosphere lasted all day with food stands and rides. I joined a long line with other children who waited to see Misty, the Palomino Pinto made famous in the 1947 children's book *Misty of Chincoteague* by Marguerite Henry. It was my favorite day of the summer. Warm sunshine. Ice cream cones. A merry-go-round ride. And ponies.

Mom pulled our suitcases from the closet two weeks later and opened them on the bed. Sadness crept in and my heart seemed to weep.

"I don't want to go home, Mom," I resisted.

She slipped a blouse off its hanger, folded it, and placed it in the bag. "Well, we have to get back. We need to take you to Lord & Taylor for back-to-school shopping while the selection of clothes is still good." She lowered the top of the suitcase and clicked the latch. Her motions were so robotic, as though her heart had been detached from her brain. I wondered if she wanted to stay, too. I despised shopping. I felt like a dog on a leash dragged from one store to another, trying on one outfit after another until Mom picked out what she liked best. I had little say in the matter except for the fur-collared winter coat I chose each fall.

I wanted to stay on the farm where I felt useful, loved, and content. I did not have playmates, but Gramps was a constant companion, and with him, I was safe. It would have been fine with me to stay there forever.

"Please, Mom! Can't we stay one more night?"

"Your father is coming home tonight. We need to be there." She did not look up as she stripped the sheets from the bed. Her words were firm, but her voice was weak. When she pursed her lips and gritted her teeth, I thought she was mad at me for wanting to stay, so I went outside to find Gramps.

*Maybe he can change her mind.*

Our suitcases were loaded in the backseat an hour later, and Mom was ready to go. Gram filled our cooler with ham salad sandwiches and a bag of freshly picked figs. She poured her concoction of fruit juices, "bug juice," we called it, into the thermos. Mom placed the cooler on the floorboard in the back, and we slid into our bucket seats. Gram and Gramps stood on the front porch as Mom put the car in gear. I rolled down the window and hung my head out, waving and waving as they grew smaller and smaller. We crept past the relic tombstones at the edge of the open acres, slipped around the bend, and I burst into tears.

"What's wrong?" Mom heard my sniffles.

"I don't want to go home. I don't want to leave. I'm afraid I won't see Gram and Gramps again," I blubbered and wiped my tears with my sleeve.

Mom tapped the brakes and looked over at me. "Do you want to go back to eat our lunch with them?"

I nodded. I was surprised by her apparent care about my feelings, but I wondered if she wanted to stay, too. At the end of the drive, Mom turned around. In an instant, my tears subsided, and my disquiet settled. We pulled back up to the house, and I lugged the thermos and cooler from the backseat. I closed the car door and looked up to see Gramps smiling, standing inside the screen door.

"Decided to come back for lunch?"

I nodded. Gram joined Gramps at the door. She noticed my tear-streaked cheeks and red eyes. "Big girls, don't cry," she grumbled as Gramps swung the door open to welcome us back.

Her words fell on me like a brick. Was I not allowed to feel sad? Did she understand my tears were for love of her? Her judgment landed on me hard, and I shut down.

Gram set the table with her multi-colored Fiestaware and ivory-handled flatware. Mom took the sandwiches from the cooler and put them on our plates while Gramps poured the bug juice into our glasses. As always, Gram said the blessing.

"Be present at our table, Lord. Be here and everywhere adored. These mercies bless and grant that we may feast in paradise with thee." John Wesley's words rattled off her tongue so fast it was hard to understand them.

We ate our lunches in silence. No one asked me why I did not want to go home. The matter was closed. No discussion was necessary. By the time our plates were cleared, my inner storm had abated, and my tears had ebbed like the tide in the Creek. Mom and I started for home again. This time, however, I sensed that we were headed into an alcohol-fueled storm of hurricane proportions.

# CHAPTER 8

Sometimes, Dad's drinking made him mellow, even jovial, until he fell asleep. Other times, it sent him into a rant over an insignificant or offhand comment. I never knew what to expect. But I was more perplexed by the rage that appeared when he had not been drinking.

Mom took me to church from the time I was a baby. As I grew, the church became an essential part of my life. I went to Sunday School, and when I was old enough, I joined the children's choir. The large Methodist Church in Westfield became a second home for me. Everyone was nice. Everyone seemed happy. I had no reason to question my safety there. But my comfort at church evaporated the day I was to receive my third-grade Bible. Dad never went to church unless I was somehow involved. His presence there that day thrilled me because I thought he was proud of me.

Thirty children lined up at the altar rail, and Pastor Hunt handed out the Bibles as the teachers read each name. Jenny Bryant. . . Scott Jones. . . Joel Marsh. . . Anne Powell. . . My anticipation grew as they drew closer to me. But, when I heard the teacher say, "Paul Segal," my enthusiasm flew out of the stained-glass window.

*You skipped me!*

The pastor and teachers moved down the line. I did not know what to do. I was afraid of embarrassing my teacher if I said a word. I stood silent and still, sure that I was invisible even as tears filled my eyes. When the last name was read, I filed into the pew behind the other children and nursed my bruised heart. I knew I had to pull out of it before church ended and Dad saw me. I knew if he saw my distress, it would set him off. Maybe if I was all right, he would be too. My effort made no difference. When worship ended and the congregants spilled into the aisles to leave, Dad grabbed my hand and pushed his way forward to the door that led through the sacristy and into the hall.

*It's not my fault!*

Terrorized by his wrath, I did not dare utter a word. He was looking for the teacher but yelled at me until he found her. "What the hell? Why didn't you get a Bible?" His voice was loud enough for my classmates and their parents to hear.

Blood rushed to my cheeks. I stood still as stone, shell-shocked, lips zipped, and wanting to crawl into my hole.

When he found the teacher, he called her out before God and everyone. "My daughter didn't get a Bible! What is wrong with you? Why didn't my daughter get a Bible?"

"I am so sorry. It was an oversight. We will get her one," she said in a calm voice before she bolted down the hall.

*How can I face her again? How can I go back to Sunday School?*

Somehow, I managed. Maybe it was because I knew it was not my mistake. Perhaps it was my tenacity that propped me up. Maybe it was Mom's determination to make sure I did not let this episode get between me and Jesus. Whatever it was, I walked back into Sunday School the next week feeling small and timid—a mouse startled by an elephant. I imagined the worst: the teacher would not want me in her class and tell me to leave. I stayed back and waited to enter the classroom until a few other children arrived.

*If I go in with them, maybe the teacher won't notice me.*

The teacher did see me, and she greeted me along with all the other children. The class went on as though nothing had happened. I heaved a sigh of relief. We heard Bible stories. We sang, "Jesus loves me, this I know." But I could not pretend it had not happened. I began to separate myself into pieces. In public, I was charming, happy, compliant—all smiles. In private, my inner world crumbled under the weight of self-doubt, self-criticism, and anxiety.

There were days after school when I took that inner world to the piano bench, where I tried to sound out familiar tunes on the keys. From that, Mom assumed I had an interest in her untouched piano. Without talking with me, she enrolled me in lessons with what she described as "the best piano teachers in the area" at The French School of Music.

"I want you to learn to play correctly," she explained.

My first lesson was the next day, providing me no window to generate excuses to talk her out of this. Dismay settled into my gut. I did not want to take piano lessons, but I had no recourse. The fifteen-minute drive was a forty-five-minute descent into hell as butterflies swarmed in my stomach. Mom parked the car along the curb in front of the school, and consternation dragged me towards the big white house with green shutters and an imposing front porch.

"My stomach hurts," I moaned and prayed she would take me home rather than up the steps.

"So does mine," she replied.

*This is not about you, and that doesn't help.*

Non-plussed, she stayed the course and escorted me through the screen door. We stood in the massive foyer, with a tall ceiling and large black-and-white linoleum floor tiles. The air hung thick with the aroma of sweet vanilla. At the far end of the room, I noticed a large, glass-front cabinet filled with trinkets. Curiosity pulled me toward it, and I stood before it in awe, examining its contents. It contained a menagerie of miniature items: ceramic dogs and cats, tiny cars and trains, glass vases, and a cuckoo clock. Captivated by the tiny world, I was drawn into fantasy when a tall, stately woman with short salt-and-pepper hair pulled open the French doors to our left.

"Jan-eese?"

I had never heard a French accent before, but with no one else in the room, I figured she was talking to me. Mom introduced us, and we followed her into a studio with rows of black folding chairs. Mme. Seguin was her name, and she motioned me up two steps and onto the black cushioned bench in front of the black grand piano. I had never seen a piano this big. It was sleek and beautiful. She sat to my right, and Mom sat in the chair in the corner to my left. Mme. Seguin placed my fingers on the white keys, raised my wrists, and placed a quarter on the back of each hand.

"This is how you will practice until you are able to hold your hands without the coins falling off," she said. She put a piece of paper on the piano in front of me, pointed at a note, and simultaneously placed my index finger on the white key in the middle of the piano.

"This is middle C."

She was patient and calm. She seemed nice, even with her firm and strict manners. She carried herself like a soldier but did not sound like one, so I decided to trust her. My reluctance waned. I sat up straight, raised my wrists, and let her carry me through my thirty-minute lesson. At the end, she picked up a small booklet and opened it to the first page. At the top, she wrote the date and placed a blue star below it.

"Come," she said.

We followed her out of the studio and back into the foyer to stand in front of the trinket-filled cabinet. Each knick-knack had a tag with a number on it. My eyes fixed on the small cuckoo clock with "100" on the card in front, and all the other kitsch in the cabinet faded into the background.

"At the end of every lesson, you will get a star in this book," she explained as she handed the book to me. "Blue is good. Red is better. Gold is best. Those numbers are how many gold stars you must get in a row to win a prize. You can choose any one you want from all of these."

*A prize? I want the best prize.*

I wanted the clock. I set my goal and was determined to get it. But in the meantime, when I played in recitals, I quickly noticed that other students displayed a measure of talent, confidence, and passion I did not possess. Their performance perfection. My fingers fumbled. They excelled in competition while my mind went blank. As time passed, my interest in piano waned. My sole motivation was to get that clock, so I stayed with it, but Mom and I never discussed it.

✧

Mom decided we should have a dog. Another decision made without conversation, but I was delighted.

*It's not a baby brother or sister, but it will do. I will have a companion.*

We found a standard dachshund puppy at a pet store and brought her home. I named her Frankie. A few months after I started piano, Mom set out to teach me a different lesson. It was springtime, and Mom said Frankie was in heat. I had no idea what that meant. One warm afternoon, someone brought another dachshund into our fenced-in backyard, and together, the three of us sat at the picnic table and drank our lemonade while the two dogs romped in the grass. About two months later, Frankie delivered six puppies in her pen under the kitchen table. The "sex talk" without words. No explanation—I was on my own to figure it out.

The kitchen smelled terrible after the puppies were born, like a skunk had strolled through the house. Nevertheless, these tiny creatures enchanted me. As they were born, I gave them "people names," and I was the only one in the family who knew which one was which. They brought out a nurturing instinct in me. They were my "babies," and I was happy to care for them—until all hell broke loose.

Mom, Dad, and I went out one afternoon. We came home to find shreds of jungle green cloth and chunks of gray foam stuffing strewn all over the house. Frankie and her puppies had escaped from the pen, out of the kitchen, and into the living room, where they had ripped the upholstery off of our brand-new sofa. When Dad saw the damage, his eyes looked as though they were about to pop out of their sockets. His face turned scarlet, and his cheeks puffed out. As he started to yell, I ran to my room. Mom spoke to him in an apologetic and submissive voice as though it had been her fault, though no one knew how they had escaped.

"I can fix it," she said. Her words calmed Dad enough to pour himself a drink and get to the brown room, where he turned on the television and turned up the volume. The rowdy ruckus of a football game seeped through the wall into my room.

For the next month, Mom cut pieces of fabric from the underside of the couch cushions and sewed them on top and around the edges with such skill that, in the end, no one could see the harm done unless they picked up the cushions and looked underneath.

Despite his volatility, I craved Dad's attention. The day he announced that he would take me on a father/daughter night on the town, I could have been thrilled. Instead, I was put off by his assumption. I did want to go, but I wanted to be invited, not told. My excitement won out when Mom bought me a beautiful silk dress with a floral print and a shimmering emerald green bolero jacket. For my ninth birthday, Dad and I went to the Copacabana, a famous New York nightclub. Paul Anka performed, and Dad, wanting to ensure everyone saw him with "his kitten," arranged for Mr. Anka to come to our table for pictures. He wanted proof positive he was a "good dad." A therapist would point out years later, "He took you to a place where he could drink." She was right, but I did not notice at the time. I had learned to embrace the rare happy moments. If he was not throwing a tantrum, I played the part of the good girl.

A few weeks later, a widespread influenza virus put all of us to bed. Dad and I soon were back on our feet, but Mom's recovery was long and uneven. By the Christmas holiday, she was back to her routine. But she suffered her first migraine headache the day I returned to school after winter break. She had four or five more in quick succession before seeing a chiropractor who prescribed traction for her neck. It became the norm for me to come home from school to find her on the couch in the brown room with her head in a cradle attached to weights, which were supposed to pull her neck muscles and relieve the tension between the vertebrae.

When she could, she kept up with her social obligations, but one by one, she had to miss a bridge game here and a College Club meeting there until all that was left was choir practice and Sunday morning church. She was to attend choir practice on a cold winter night, but Dad was held up at work. So, she phoned Ruth across the street to see if her elderly mother could stay with me for an hour. Peggy stepped with caution down their driveway and started up the steep hill to our house. As she climbed, she slipped, cracked open her head, and arrived on our front porch with a gash on her forehead and blood streaming down her face. Mom gathered every towel she could find to staunch the bleeding. Instead of heading to choir practice, she herded us all to the car, and we sped off to the emergency room, leaving a pile of bloody towels on the kitchen floor. In her rush, Mom failed to leave Dad a note. When he arrived home, he saw the towels and assumed it was my blood on them. By the time we got back, his alcohol-fed rage spewed at Mom like a sliced artery. I retreated to my room, but his histrionics bled through the wall into my bedroom.

The traction therapy relieved Mom's migraines for a few months, but its effectiveness dwindled by the summer, and her headaches persisted. She hired a housekeeper. Dad stayed at work. No one talked about her declining health or the hole it was creating—an eddy, that drained the family of its lifeblood.

# CHAPTER 9

Aunt Mary, Gramps' sister, lived with Gram and Gramps for about six years. She was frequently my playmate on rainy days. Perched on her hunter green couch, and I on a topaz brown ottoman, with a leather-covered game table between us, she taught me to play Crazy Eights, Go Fish, and double solitaire. Before retiring, she had a career as a professional administrator in a government agency in Washington, DC. She never married. With her slight frame and her snow-white hair in tiny curls, she did not intimidate me. In her presence, I felt comfortable and wanted. I never doubted her care for me. So, it came as a huge shock when we returned to the Shore in the spring, and I learned that she had moved back to Washington to be near friends, her sister, nieces, and nephews. Mi abuela disappeared from my life, and now Aunt Mary was gone. Without warning, it seemed like a Band-Aid ripped off. I needed information.

"Why did Aunt Mary leave?" I pressed Gram.

"Oh, she's just an old spinster," she said, her dismissive voice crackling like the Wicked Witch of the West. Her tone let me know she would field no more questions about my Aunt Mary. She had no interest in hearing about my loss.

"What is a spinster?"

"An unmarried woman." Her words were clipped.

She said it like it was a disease, a judgment defining what, not who, Aunt Mary was. I did not care that she had never been married or had children. She and Gramps were the two adults who made me feel valued. She never shooed me away or spoke a harsh word to me. She never made me feel embarrassed or ashamed. I was going to miss her a lot.

I was old enough now to want to play with other children during our extended visits to the farm. And now, with Aunt Mary gone, Mom and Gram knew they had to find a counter to my solitude. A nearby farmer had three sons and a daughter. Molly was about my age, and her brother, Danny, was a year older. Gram arranged a playdate for me at their house midway into the summer. They lived on a working farm with hogs, chickens, and horses. I was eager to spend the afternoon with them. Gram dropped me off, and Molly and Danny took me straight away to the animals. We took slop to the hogs, collected eggs from the hen house, and fed apples to the horses. All of this was new to me. A whole new, fascinating world. But it was hard work, and it was more work than play. When Gram picked me up, I was so tired I fell asleep on the five-minute drive back to our farm.

Gram drove me back to Molly and Danny's house a few weeks later so she and Mom could go shopping. Up the sandy drive, past the hog sty, Gram inched the car towards the house, dodging the free-range chickens. At the house, she stopped the car, and I put my hand on the door handle to get out. She turned and scolded me. "Don't you play doctor while you are here. Do you understand?"

Her mandate came out of nowhere. I had no idea what caused her to say it, but her words made me so uncomfortable I jumped out of the car and slammed the door behind me. I wondered what it was about but knew better than to expect an explanation. I was reluctant to go back to Molly's after that, worried I might do something Gram would disapprove of.

Gram's voice was different now, more critical. She articulated her opinions in my presence more often, making me jittery inside when I thought her judgment would fall on me. I noticed she was very particular: how the dishes were washed and dried, how the clothes were hung, and how, each evening, she laid out the next day's clothes for Gramps to wear. If all was not done as she expected, she quickly let us know and expected us to make corrections. Fearing her disfavor, I began to distance myself from her.

One afternoon, Gramps and I went to pick up Miss Hattie. She had a warm smile with tobacco-stained teeth; her dark face made them look whiter than they were. Her yellow dress with white flowers was clean and pressed. Her kinky salt-and-pepper hair was pulled tight into a bun and covered with a red and white bandana. She opened the car door behind me, slung her bag in first, and sunk into the backseat. I wondered what was in the bag.

*Is that a purse or a lunch bag?*

It was none of my business, so I did not ask. Gramps barely said "hello" when she got in the car, so I supposed I was not to speak to her at all. She sat in silence for the ten-minute ride to the farm. Once there, she went straight to work. We did not see her or hear a sound except for the whirr of the vacuum cleaner.

Gram, Gramps, Mom, and I sat at the dining room table for lunch at noon. Sliced country ham, rolls, and what Gramps called stinky cheese. It did stink—like a sewer. After lunch, we cleaned our plates, but Gram left food on the table and put a clean plate, fork, and knife at her place.

"Hattie, you can come for lunch now," she hollered up the stairs.

*What?*

"Gram, why didn't Miss Hattie have lunch with us?" I was baffled. There was an empty chair at the table. She could have eaten with us.

"It's not what we do."

*Whoa.*

I moved from confusion to anger. Miss Hattie was a woman who, except for the color of her skin and the way she talked, seemed to me to be much like Gram. I thought Miss Hattie should have eaten her lunch with us and that Gram was being cruel. Gramps tried to assuage me with the story of the first time Mom had seen a black man and wanted to know why his face was so dirty. It did not impress me. In Miss Hattie, I saw a kind, gentle, and helpful woman who deserved respect rather than second-class treatment. But it was not up to me to decide who sat and ate with us. I did not like how she was treated, but the good girl kept her mouth shut.

By the end of our summer visit, I had had enough of what I thought were unkind opinions about or the treatment of others. There were no tears this time as Mom and I packed up and started our drive back north. Nevertheless, in my gut, I knew that whether I stayed on the farm or went home, my life would always be defined by someone else's anger.

# CHAPTER 10

# What Gram Taught Me

Crabbing requires patience and skill.
The proof was in the catch netted on a given afternoon.
Anxiety or restlessness results in an empty takeaway.
Calm and patience yield better results.
Impatience results in disappointment.

🦀

Big girls don't cry.
*I wondered who made that rule.*

🦀

Your body is the source of sin and shame.
*It was a Victorian-era value that she delivered*
*in edicts without rationale or conversation.*
*It was easier to absorb the lesson than make sense of it.*

🦀

P-E-C-A-N is pronounced peh-cahn.
The other pronunciation, pee-can, is a toilet.
Or, on boat days, it was the empty coffee tin at the back of the boat.

🦀

Only some are worthy to feast at the table.
Cardinals, chickadees, titmice, warblers, wrens,
scarlet tanagers, bluebirds, robins, even blue jays
were welcome at the feeders outside the dining room window.
Grackles were dirty, greedy bullies who scared away the others.
When they dared to perch at the feeders, they were shooed away.

❦

The world is black and white—no shades of gray.
Things are right, or they are wrong.
There is no middle ground.

❦

God will get you if you don't watch out.
God is angry, vengeful, and mean.
Life should be lived without provoking God and forfeiting a ticket to heaven.
Everyone should believe this and live accordingly.

# CHAPTER 11

I was home from school with an undiagnosed case of mouth sores, a fever, and swollen glands, watching Password on TV in the brown room when breaking news interrupted the program. President Kennedy had been shot. The country went into turmoil, but I was focused on the turbulence growing in my ten-year-old life. Something was making me sick. No one seemed to notice or care.

Dad and I shared the full bathroom with a short wall that separated the toilet from the bathtub. As far back as I could remember, Dad had the habit of coming into the bathroom to relieve himself when I was in the tub. I was ten years old the night I lay in the bottom of the tub for a long time, expecting he would come in at any moment. My fingertips had turned to prunes. The water had cooled. Goosebumps popped up on my arms. I was getting cold when it hit me: he was not coming.

*What had I done wrong?*

I gave up, sat up, pulled the plug from the drain, stepped out of the tub onto the bathmat, dried myself off, and went to my room. A piece of rotten produce thrown into the trash. I wept from the sting of rejection. I crawled into bed, pulled up the covers, curled into a fetal position, and sucked my thumb for comfort. Even Dad's ridicule had not shaken me of the habit.

"You'll get buck teeth. You'll walk down the aisle in your wedding gown with your thumb in your mouth."

His taunting could not separate me from the one thing that soothed my nervousness, but something finally did. We traveled to the farm for Thanksgiving weekend. On Friday night, I was asleep in my bed in Gram and Gramps' room with my thumb in my mouth. I had not heard them come into the room but awoke when I heard Gram's voice.

"When will she stop? It's awful."

Her words jarred me. A door slammed in my face. Her judgment yanked the thumb from between my teeth, never to return. Mission accomplished. If anyone noticed, they never said a word.

After two years of piano lessons, my notebook was filled with enough gold stars to secure the cuckoo clock. I counted them page by page. One hundred.

*I did it!*

At the end of my next lesson, I told Mme. Seguin I was ready to collect my clock. She counted the stars, too, and when she reached the last one, her smile spoke of her success as much as it did mine. We walked into the foyer and up to the cabinet. She took the key from her pocket, unlocked the glass door, lifted the clock from its hook, and handed it to me. I beamed. She seemed proud of what we had accomplished together.

I held the clock like a newborn chick in my lap as Mom drove without uttering a word. At home, I tossed my sheet music on the piano bench and went to my room to decide where to hang my clock. Over my bed, where I could see it—a reminder of my accomplishment. Then, I went to the brown room where Mom was resting.

"I want to quit piano now, " I said with a newfound confidence. I was tired of daily practice. It had become a vacuum that sucked the joy from my afternoons. Recitals and competitions left me embarrassed. Playing the piano was less enjoyable to me than feeding slop to Molly's hogs.

"Well, you can't. You can't quit. You are too good. You can be a piano teacher." She was unconvincing.

I may have been good, but I was not good enough. If she knew how performing tied me in knots, how it fed my fear of failure and embarrassment, how miserable it made me, she did not care. I knew what she was doing. She had come to terms with her own hostage situation, stuck at home with me and a paltry sixty dollars per month "allowance" that Dad gave her for groceries and clothes. She thought when I grew up and married, I could be content if I had the ability to earn some spending money. But she did not know me at all.

We went back and forth, our voices interweaving like the harmonious notes of a Bach minor fugue, but she would not budge. We argued until the notes became a dissonant mess, and I gave up. I saw no way to win this battle.

"I'll let you stop when you are thirteen," she said.

*Three more years?*

I could not believe my ears nor understand why this was her decision and not mine. But the compliant child saw no way out. The thought of what would happen if I refused to practice or go to a lesson terrified me.

Every minute spent on the bench was painful. If I complained, Mom reminded me of the good money they had spent on those lessons. I made my way to Chopin, Beethoven, and Liszt.

Then, the day I decided to make the best of a bad situation turned into a disaster. I prepared a couple of hymns to play when everyone gathered for Thanksgiving dinner. Mom was in the kitchen stuffing the turkey while I practiced. Dad came into the living room, put his hand on the top of the piano, and glared down at me.

"No one is going to want to listen to you play." His voice was a loud, discordant bass note that spiraled down my spine.

I stood up, went to my room and closed the door as tears poured out. I prepared to crawl into my hole, curl up in a ball, and die. The last thing I wanted to do was eat—my stomach churned. My mind disassociated—unrelated random black notes on a musician's score.

*Why did he do that? Why doesn't he encourage me or support me? Why does he always get mad at me? Why can't he see that he hurts my feelings?*

Mom's headaches became more frequent, each one more disabling. She spent days on the couch or in bed. Dad grew impatient with her and told her she needed to find a doctor to figure out what was wrong with her. After starting her search in New York with the "best" doctors who gave no diagnosis, she expanded her search to clinics across the country. She flew to Minnesota, Chicago, and Cleveland in hopes of finding someone who would give her a diagnosis. To no avail. When she was away, she arranged for someone to be home each afternoon when I arrived from school, but I never knew who would be there. A neighbor? Someone from church? A friend from one of her social clubs? They were there to greet me, help me with my homework, and have dinner ready for Dad. But he decried the arrangement and yelled at me as though I was to blame. He was indignant about having a "stranger" in his house, more agitated about his discomfort than worried about my safety or care.

*What is your problem?*

The time we spent at the farm was abbreviated that summer. Between Mom's illness and her search for a cure, we were homebound by the end of June. Mom suggested we go to Mountainside to see the fireworks for the Fourth of July. She invited a neighbor and her three sons to join us. We all piled into our station wagon and drove to the park, where we watched the light show erupt over the hillside. Everyone had a good time, I thought. But, when we got home, I learned that Mom had an experience quite different from mine.

"Mrs. O could not believe you spoke to me that way."

I had no idea what she was talking about, and she did not explain. Instead, she poured her humiliation over me, where it sank into my skin—a tick burrowing in to suck my blood.

Before I started sixth grade, I was stuffing down my anger while taking on more responsibility for my parents. Dad's drinking was out of control now. Mom's depression was growing deeper and darker. I was bearing the burden of it. Their neediness was too heavy for me to carry. Caring for them in their illnesses. Protecting the family secret. With each offense, I dug my hole deeper and withdrew further into myself.

# CHAPTER 12

## Molting

A fragile, paper-thin, gray-white husk hung from the rafter in barn one above the car's hood. Another was on the backseat, and yet another was on the barn floor stretched out across the sawdust.

"Snake skins," Gramps explained.

He picked up the one from the car seat and laid it on his workbench. We examined the two feet of thin, delicate, crunchy casing that once belonged to a black snake. The honeycomb pattern was still intact.

"The shed is longer than the snake itself. This remnant covered the top and bottom of every one of the snake's scales. Since this is all one piece, we can guess the snake was half this long."

*I want to squirm out of my skin and grow into one that fits me better.*

Scores of fragile brown insect shells held tentatively onto the bark of the black locust trees as though their lives depended on it. But they were empty, every last one. A zipper along the back of each casing set them free.

"Why do they leave their shells, Gramps?"

"The cicadas are molting. They're moving from one stage of growth to the next. This hard shell, their exoskeleton, has become too small. They need a bigger one."

Escape hatch zippers, evidence that the casing, which once held them captive, no longer suited them.

*I want to trade in my shell for a new one.*

On the piling at the end of the dock, a crab flinches at my shadow as I bend down to look closer. My presence does not stop him from munching on his barnacle lunch. But I notice under him, he harbors a mate.

"Gramps, what's going on?"

"Oh, the crab on top protects the one underneath shedding its shell. They call it a "double" because if you can catch them, it is two for the price of one. The shell of the one on top is hard, but the one on the underside is a "peeler," getting ready to lose his outer shell. Once that happens, what is left is a soft-shell crab needing the shelter of another to keep him safe. There, underneath his mate, he is shielded from predators. When the outer shell is hardened, they will go their separate ways."

*I wish I had a protector so I could grow a new hard shell.*

---

Gram's two yellow canaries in the dining room looked sick. The bottom of the cage was covered with dull, yellow feathers. Their singing was muted. Their activity was subdued. Even the cuttlefish hanging on the bars of the cage was untouched. They were ghosts, but Gram assured me they were fine.

"They're molting. In a few weeks, they will have soft, fluffy, yellow feathers and look the same as before."

Sure enough, when we visited the next month, the canaries had returned to themselves. Bright yellow feathers. Chipper. Appetite returned. Chirping away the day.

*I need a new coat. A new life. Please, God.*

# CHAPTER 13

The morning of my thirteenth birthday, I smelled freedom in the air. I did not take a successful outcome for granted, so I planned my strategic approach, waiting until after school to raise the subject. I was ready when I got off the bus and walked in the door. I slipped off my blue raincoat and hung it on the hook in the mudroom to drip dry. My shoes were wet, too, so I left them in the garage. It had been raining all day, but the weather did not dampen my resolve. I dropped my books on the dining room table and went straight to the brown room. Mom was on the couch in the throes of another migraine. Her eyes were closed, but when she grunted, "Hello," I knew she was awake. Headache or not, I was determined to state my request, no—my demand. I had done as she expected: plowed my way through five grueling years of daily practice, with the occasional bombed recital or failed competition thrown in. I was done.

"Go practice your piano lesson," she whispered.

"Nope. I'm done. I quit!"

She raised herself to sit up and adjusted the ice pack on the back of her neck.

"What are you talking about?"

"You told me I could stop taking piano lessons when I turned thirteen. That's today."

"I never said that."

"Well, you did. Give me one reason, one good reason." I needed a reason, like a plant needs air to survive.

*You don't have one.*

I demanded an answer and refused to concede until I got one.

At last, she spit it out. "I took piano lessons for two years, and my mother let me quit. I regret my decision to this day, and I won't let you make the same mistake."

*Why did you buy that piano?*

"But you said..."

"I never said you could quit."

*Why was I the only one who remembered that?*

～

School, like church, was a haven for me. A place where I had friends and teachers who seemed to care about me. Now that I was in junior high school, my circle of friends had grown, and I invited some of them to the house to celebrate my thirteenth birthday. They came for games, snacks, music, and cake on Saturday. We filled the French café-themed rec room with laughter and song. Toward the end of the evening, the boys got a little rowdy and started jumping to the music. At some point, Tom, who was tall for his age, went up into the air. His feet left the floor—a basketball player leaping to tip the ball into the net. He stretched his arm high above his head, and with a massive grin, he powered his fist through a ceiling tile. The smashed tile landed with a thud on the green felt carpet, and a cloud of dust encircled Tom's feet. The room fell silent for a second before we all burst out laughing.

After all the guests left, Dad came downstairs to help me clean up. When he saw the mess on the floor and the hole in the ceiling, he went ballistic. His anger could have shattered the rest of the ceiling. He was drunk. He screamed at me louder than ever before.

I had enough. I was no longer willing to serve as a target for his irrational, alcohol-fueled rampages. "I didn't do this. Do NOT blame me. This is no way to treat me on my birthday."

He was shocked when he realized his rage had unleashed my own fury. He looked stunned, as though he had been caught committing a crime. His compliant little girl talked back. I did not stick around to see if my words had any effect or if he was at all contrite. I said my peace and bolted up the stairs to seek refuge in my room.

*I stood up for myself! I actually stood up to him!*

Sitting on the side of my bed, I hugged my pillow tight to my chest and rocked back and forth to soothe my nervous stomach. In the mirror across my room, I saw a brave young girl. Yes, a wave of guilt crashed against the shores of my conscience, and I was still petrified that his anger would swallow me whole. But the longer I stared at the girl in the mirror, the more confident I was that I was not to blame. I was not guilty. My core felt solid.

Self-assurance was essential now because I knew I was on my own. Mom was away as often as Dad was. When she was home, she was too sick to defend or protect me. She would not have my back; she did not have the strength. I knew standing up to him would be easier said than done. He had always intimidated me, a perception that intensified with his drinking. I could never assume I would be able to calm him down with my words, and sometimes, the situation before me was too bewildering for a thirteen-year-old to sort out on her own.

One evening the following spring, my parents hosted a dinner party in our New Jersey home before we moved to Northern Virginia. The revelry went late into the night; the noise increased in proportion to the amount of alcohol consumed. I was supposed to be asleep in my bed, but there was too much noise. As I lay on my back, staring at the ceiling, I heard moaning from the brown room. It sounded like someone was sick and I worried that it might be Mom. My curiosity rose as the noise continued until it got the best of me. I tossed back my covers and stepped from my room into the hallway. I peeked around the doorframe into the brown room.

The light on the table in the corner cast an eerie glow. Dad's white, collared shirt was untucked and unbuttoned, revealing his ribbed undershirt and a glimpse of his belly. His dark gray slacks sagged as he rolled around on the floor. The woman in his arms wore a flimsy pink dress, her belt unlatched, her dress slipped over her shoulders. She had shed her shoes in what was a passionate, sexual embrace. Dad was drunk and making out with her, one hand reaching down into her dress. The two appeared melded together—melted wax around a candlestick.

*That is not Mom. This is wrong.*

Just as I put the pieces together, Mom, who stood at the end of the hallway, rushed towards me and pushed me into my room.

"Get back in bed! Go to sleep!" she whispered a loud "sh" and closed the door behind her.

I climbed back into my bed and, alone in the dark, attempted to process the scene that haunted me. There was no erasing from my mind what I had seen, nor could I tune out the sighs that still oozed through the wall. All I could think of was gooey, sticky sap seeping from a tree trunk. Sleep eluded me until the guests began to retrieve their coats, and finally, the house grew quiet. I was left with my confused and fear-filled thoughts until I fell asleep.

*What will happen tomorrow? Will Mom stay? If she leaves, will she take me with her? We would be better if she and I left.*

Mom and Dad cleaned up the house the next morning, seemingly oblivious to the one mess he had made, a mess no amount of scrubbing would erase.

# CHAPTER 14

# Infestation

Oblivious to the presence of occupants in the farmhouse, the mice took up residency in every room. No longer restricted to the barns, they found their way into the warmth. They stole stuffing from pillows to build nests in desk drawers and coat sleeves. They left their calling card droppings in the drinking glasses in the pantry and the frying pans under the cooktop. They shredded upholstery on couches and chairs. A party gone awry. And the air that once held the promise of homemade clam chowder or freshly baked brownies now hung thick with the dust of microscopic, asthma-inducing dander.

Meanwhile, assuming no one would notice, the black snakes took up residency in the black locust tree between the farmhouse and the cove. Dozens of them draped over the branches, like children dangling from monkey bars. The numbers were so thick one wondered how the branches could hold them all. And the air that once reeked of muddy low tide now carried an unspoken message to anyone repelled by their presence: NO TRESPASSING.

Lies now grew in frequency and substance. Cancerous. Untreated, they burrowed their way into the family system. Despite the symptoms, which were plain to see, no one questioned the metastasis. No one asked Dad anymore where he was or who he was with. He had become an enigma cloaked in alcohol and rage. There was evidence to confront his stories, but no one ever did. Our job was to keep his secrets close—all of them—and we did. The less we knew, the better. The dark cloud bank foreboding an epic storm brewed on the horizon and left scars on the landscape of my identity.

# CHAPTER 15

Mom and I crammed the last of our belongings into the back seat of her new turquoise convertible Karmann Ghia. The weather was hot and muggy as she backed the car down our driveway for the last time. We were headed to our new home in Reston, Virginia. Dad started his new job the week before and was already there.

I sensed Mom's sadness in her silence. Her loss was palpable. Grief seeped from her heart and was caught by the wind to cycle back and take hold of her again. In contrast to her melancholy, I was full of anticipation, eager for a fresh start. New Jersey had always felt uncomfortable to me. I looked forward to making new friends. Plus, I was naïve enough to think this could be a new beginning for Mom and Dad. I longed for them to find a way through what I made myself believe was their rough patch. In my gut, I knew better. I knew their marriage was beyond repair, but I was smart enough to know it was not mine to fix. My job was to settle into high school, to find new friends, and to make my home here.

Mom sped down the turnpike, and I thought of Dorothy as she traveled the yellow brick road with her friends. "There's no place like home," she chanted. Dorothy longed for home. I was unsure if I wanted the one I was relegated to. But I had nowhere else to go, so I determined to make the best of it, to build my own community away from the dysfunction under my roof. The problem was that I carried the internalized message that the world is a dangerous place. Did I dare trust it now? The farm, church, and school were the exceptions to the rule. They were my places of refuge. The natural world of the farm embraced me and held me close. Church people were kind and trustworthy. School teachers welcomed and encouraged me. I sensed that I would be okay with new friends, a church family, and caring teachers.

As the car crested the driveway at our new house, a group of teenagers walked around the corner.

*Finding new friends should be pretty easy.*

I soon learned that the high school I would attend was brand new. That meant that all the students would explore this new territory together. I sensed that I was where I needed to be. Opening a fresh chapter in an unread book, moving from chaos to calm. I was happy for what seemed like the first time in my life.

Despite my efforts to find happiness, the discord at home overshadowed my joy. Dad almost never came home anymore. When he did, he was either drunk or sick. A hangover. Pleurisy. Pneumonia. The abuse of his body was apparent. Yellow eyes. Pale gray face. Blue fingertips. Stumbling down the stairs. He never hinted that anything was wrong, but in his medicine cabinet I saw drugs for high blood pressure and diabetes.

Mom's condition worsened by the week. Her depression darkened one day at a time. She was retreating into a hole of her own making, sleeping away the days or begging doctors for a diagnosis. Between the loss of her community and watching her marriage unravel, any joy she once had was melting away. I did not recognize her anymore. She had not been the most nurturing mother, but between her and Dad, I cleaved to her as the stable one. She was my life raft. Now, any sanity she had to offer me was fading from sight.

I came to despise the rare occasion when they were both at home. The chill in the house was as icy as a walk-in freezer. Their cold war drove me to the homes of friends or the silo of my bedroom with the volume turned up on my radio.

*Leave me out of your battles.*

Mom's old black pedal Singer sewing machine gathered dust in the basement, so I wiped off the case and took it to my room. I cleaned the lint from the needle plate and gave it a few drops of oil. I shopped for sunny-colored broadcloth prints and plaid wools and started sewing my own clothes as a distraction from the cold war. I filled my closet with dresses, jumpers, and suits.

One Saturday morning, I was sewing a seam on a black skirt when Dad tapped on my bedroom door.

"I'll turn it down," I huffed and reached for the knob on the radio as he opened the door uninvited.

"Pack up that old machine. I want to take you to get a new one."

*Wow. How nice!*

I had never complained about the Singer. It served me well, and I did not need a new one. But I was not about to turn down what seemed to be a generous offer. I finished the stitching, closed the case, and pulled on my jacket. I placed the machine on the floorboard in the backseat of Dad's green Chevy Nova and climbed into the front seat next to him.

A store at the new Tyson's Corner Mall displayed all makes and models of sewing machines. There were so many choices! It was almost overwhelming.

"Whatever you want. Pick one," Dad said.

I could have spent a considerable amount of time wondering why he was present and generous, but the options overcame me, and I knew I had to make a decision. I knew better than to trust his good mood and thought it best to get this done and get home before he got pissed off and changed his mind.

Without delay, I chose a machine in a sleek, slick, baby-blue plastic case. It appealed to me because it had a zigzag stitch feature.

*I can make buttonholes!*

The next day, Mom returned from her trip to a Florida clinic, and my exuberance over my new machine was short-circuited when she noticed it on the table in my room.

"Where's my sewing machine?"

"Dad took me to the Singer store at the mall. We traded it for this new one."

Her face turned beet red. "Get…in…the…car!"

*Oh. Oh no. I see it now. I am a pawn in their war game.*

I knew I was not to blame. I was the innocent victim—collateral damage. Still, I was ashamed to be the unknowing accomplice—guilty of aiding and abetting a robbery. The ride to the mall was twenty minutes of unbearable silence that was pushing me closer to a breaking point.

*What was Dad thinking? What was I thinking? How much longer can I live like this?*

In less than a minute, Mom found her machine on the store floor, lined up with other black cases—soldiers in formation awaiting orders. I wondered if any of them arrived as mine had, victims of a stealth attack. She handed the store clerk a wad of cash, picked up the case, yanked my arm, and pulled me out of the store. To her credit, she did not yell at me. She understood I was not to blame, but she was not inclined to relieve me of the heavy armor of guilt weighing me down.

Dad's ploy of putting me in the middle was not new. What was new was my awareness of his tricks. I was on to him now. I had to be vigilant and protect myself. I could not take care of Mom—that was her job.

Standing before my mirror one morning, I noticed a lump in the center of my forehead. It had appeared out of nowhere overnight. It was not red, did not itch, and did not seem to be a bug bite. But I feared I would soon look like a unicorn if it grew any more. Mom took me to a dermatologist. After several x-rays and no diagnosis, he recommended it be surgically removed.

When Dad heard the plan, he flew into orbit. "No one is putting a scalpel anywhere near my daughter's face," he shouted.

*I am in the middle of your war again. Damn it!*

Mom stepped back as he scoured the medical community to find another doctor. Instead of surgery, Dad found a doctor who put me on a low-fat diet and prescribed a unique facial exfoliant and light therapy. To everyone's relief, the lump was gone in two months. I did not want to give up hot dogs and French fries, but I preferred a restrictive diet to a deformed face.

Dad won that power struggle with Mom, but the victory gave him license to take me somewhere I was unprepared to go.

"You have a doctor's appointment tomorrow afternoon. I'll pick you up from school."

Per his instruction, which was more like an order, I was standing in front of the school the next afternoon when he drove up.

"Where are we going?"

"We are going to see a doctor in the city. You need to be protected."

*From what?*

As a kid, we traveled to vacation locations that required vaccinations against yellow fever and other tropical diseases. I thought he might surprise us with another trip. Still, I had an uneasy sense about this. We arrived in northwest DC, and Dad parked the car on the street. We walked around the corner to a brownstone building and up two flights of stairs to a doctor's office. We waited in the cold, dark reception area until a nurse opened the door and called my name. I followed her to an exam room.

"Get undressed. Put this on. It ties in the back." She sounded like a drill sergeant. The door slammed behind her.

*I don't think I'm getting a shot.*

When you don't know what you don't know, you don't know what or who to ask. So, I did as the nurse commanded, stepped up to sit on the cold table, and waited—a soldier awaiting orders.

The doctor, in his white coat, waltzed in, chart in hand. He was an older man with a kind, round face, and a bald crown.

"Do you want someone in here with you?"

I shrugged. "Well, I don't know what's happening, so I don't know."

He stuck his head out the exam room door and called in the nurse, who came and stood by my side. Without saying a word, the doctor gave me my first pelvic exam, and I was horrified. Exposed like a naked baby and treated like one—too young to be brought in on the conversation. I was violated. I put on my clothes and stuffed my embarrassment down my throat. The nurse handed me a paper bag on my way out the door. Dad did not say a word to me as we drove home, and I, too, was silent, my tongue left on the exam room floor.

In the privacy of my bedroom, I opened the bag. Pamphlets. Condoms. I was clueless about what to do with them and was not about to ask—I had been traumatized enough for one day. I wanted no part of this, so I threw the bag in the trash. My confusion and shame lingered long after the garbage went to the curb.

My innocence was shattered on a regular basis now, and I had no one to help me make sense of it. My self-constructed hole that had protected me for fifteen years was leaking, and I was no longer safe.

*What am I going to do? I have no place to go. I don't know how to cope anymore.*

I buried myself in my books. I distracted myself with sewing. I stayed away from home as much as I could. What else could I do? One of them was always sick, and they expected me to care for them. The more care I gave, the more my resentment grew. My once-healthy detachment was now full-blown self-protective disassociation. A perfect storm gathered around me. I no longer knew how to avoid being swallowed whole by their violent vocal vortex. I obsessed over how this would end and how to protect myself before, during, and after the last battle. One day, it came to this.

"If your mother and I divorced, who would you live with?"

*Oh my God. Did you really say that?*

There was no way in hell I was going to live with him, but because I was afraid of his wrath, I did not dare say so. Staying with Mom was the safer alternative, but I knew better than to say that. Leaving the room was my only option. So, I turned towards the kitchen. "I don't know," I mumbled and darted to my room.

From the time of the incident of infidelity in New Jersey, I no longer tolerated his behavior, and he knew it. I disapproved of the lie he was living and despised that he seemed intent on dragging me down with him. I wanted him to leave and not return—leave me to enjoy my friends, school, and teenage life. It was true Mom was sick and getting worse. And she was manipulative. But she was also heartbroken—anyone could see that. It mattered less to me that her misery adhered to me like a wet dress.

There was a price to pay for such loyalty, though. In her pain, she still could not allow me to chart my own path or find joy in my passions. She found another piano teacher in Maryland and carted me halfway around the beltway to Rose's living room every Thursday evening. She took advantage of the forty-minute drive each way to pour ice water on what I cared most about.

"Why do you bother with cheerleading? There is no future there."

After weeks of practice and a less-than-perfect tryout, I had made the junior varsity squad. My knee buckled on a landing mid-routine, but I regained my balance and continued my effort. My name was the last to be called, but I was riding high on a cloud when I approached one of the judges afterward.

"How did I survive the cut after that misstep?"

"You kept going."

Her words revealed a part of me I had not been aware of—I was strong.

*I kept going. That's all it took. I will fall again, but all I have to do is keep going.*

Mom did not care one bit. She followed her fantasy and tried to fix her past by keeping me glued to the piano bench. In spite of her, and perhaps to spite her, I resolved to stay afloat, clinging to the raft of what little sanity I could carve out for myself at school and with friends. Academically, I competed against myself—I no longer cared what Mom or Dad thought of my grades. I was determined to do my best for myself, not for them. Their vicious verbiage eventually devolved into ugly notes left on the kitchen counter. I lived every day between the proverbial rock and hard place while their battle raged around me.

# CHAPTER 16

# Messages My Father Gave Me

Do as I say, not as I do.
Be a good girl and pay no attention to my mixed messages.
*How am I to tolerate your hypocrisy?*

🕊

Those who can't do, teach.
If you can do something, do it.
*How can someone teach something they cannot do?*

🕊

It is a woman's prerogative to change her mind.
And make no mistake, I will not change mine.
*How can I trust my insights and abilities if they are subject to change?*

🕊

Rage is a powerful tool for controlling people.
That is how you will get what you want.
*How can I get what I need without being angry?*

🕊

You can be whatever you want to be.
Take it from me: an immigrant who achieved the American dream.
*I can't be a teacher, though, can I?*

🕊

Above all, be loyal to yourself.
Trust no one but yourself.
*How can I have a healthy relationship this way?*

# CHAPTER 17

I refused to collapse or surrender to the increased tension at home. I faced each day without considering the chaos that might erupt at any moment. I compartmentalized my life and kept my friendships and academics separate from home. It was a bifurcated existence that I managed the best I could. Life perked along, one day to the next, without much drama. It did not mean there was no catastrophe looming. It meant I was oblivious, like the person walking down the street who fails to anticipate the pavement underneath her feet give way without warning, even though she knows it is possible. When the earthquake hits, glasses and plates fall from shelves. Bookcases topple over. Structures crumble, and people are crushed beneath their weight. Unbeknownst to me, a seismic shift was in the making.

I hustled Mom from bed the day I turned sixteen, and we drove to the Department of Motor Vehicles. The driver's license represented liberation to me—from the chains of caretaking and nail-biting. After passing the test, I dropped Mom at home and went to school. That afternoon, I presented my case to her: why I should be allowed to drive to school every day. No teenager wants to ride a school bus if they can help it. I was no exception.

"You won't have to pick me up after cheerleading practice. I can pick up groceries on my way home. I can run errands for you."

She countered every point of persuasion I advanced. She pushed back on every angle of what I believed to be an open and shut case. But in the middle of her last argument, she started to stomp her feet like a two-year-old having a tantrum.

*Are you really going to act like a child about this?*

"It's not the driving of mechanics," she said. "It's the mechanics of driving."

"What are you talking about?"

Her mind often went to analytics—it was her math background—but this made no sense. I was baffled. Before I could extract more information from her, her body tensed. Her hands balled into fists. Her face grew red, and I thought she was holding her breath, preparing for her last assault. But then her eyes rolled back in her head, and a gurgling noise emanated from her throat. When her head flew back, her entire body began to shake, and she fell to the floor in spasms.

Panic coursed through every cell in my body. I was petrified, but I knew I had to move. I ran next door and asked the neighbor to call 911. I ran back into the kitchen and found Mom regaining consciousness. By the time the ambulance arrived, she was sitting up, blood from her bitten tongue dripping from her chin. Her speech was garbled. The medics took her vitals, put her on a stretcher, and drove her to the hospital. I gathered my purse and jacket, jumped into the car, and followed, all the way blaming myself and wondering if I had caused this.

The triage nurse asked me scores of questions I could not answer. What I witnessed fractured my consciousness and swallowed whole my ability to provide her with details. A nurse's aide rolled Mom away in a wheelchair for X-rays and an EEG. When they brought her back, they attached her to a cardiac monitor. A nurse came in and drew tubes of blood before she closed the curtain and left the two of us alone. It seemed I had left my words at home on the kitchen counter. I was numb and did not know what to say.

I suspect Mom did not know what to say either. She closed her eyes and drifted off to sleep. There was no question I was conflicted about my relationship with her, but now I was beginning to realize that, in no small way, she had been my sanctuary, my shelter in a prolonged and vicious storm. This episode shattered what little safety and security she had afforded me over the years. I could not see into the future, but I knew she was less available to me now than ever.

When the test results were in, the doctor pulled back the curtain and stood at the end of the bed. "You have suffered a grand mal seizure. We will admit you for additional tests and observation."

I do not remember phoning Dad, but I must have. Later that evening, he arrived at her bedside as I told her about dissecting frogs in biology class. At eight o'clock, a voice over the intercom announced the end of visiting hours. Dad and I said goodnight to Mom and took the elevator to the parking garage. The second I stepped out of the elevator, he blew up.

"Why don't you talk to me? Why don't you tell ME about your life? Why are you always talking to your mother and not to me?"

He sounded like a five-year-old. I knew better than to react.

*You're never home? No, don't say that.*
*You don't care? No, don't say that.*
*You're kidding? No, don't say that either.*

I let him yell, hoping someone would appear and cause him to temper his rage, but I arrived at my car before anyone showed up. I contorted every muscle on my face wanting to convey what I was thinking: "What the hell is wrong with you?" I got in my car and drove off.

He was determined to continue the confrontation at home and resumed piling on as soon as we walked into the kitchen. I refused to engage. I went to my room and shut the door. The next morning, it was the stink of his stale cigarette smoke seeping under my door that woke me up.

*He's still here.*

I rolled over and stayed in bed until I heard the car back out of the driveway.

Two days later, I picked up Mom from the hospital. Her discharge papers failed to reveal a cause for the seizure. They found no connection to her headaches. They gave her a prescription for Dilantin and sent her home. For the next several months, I walked on eggshells. I did not blame myself for her seizure, but I could not shake the thought that I might set off another one.

🐦

Mom was no closer to a diagnosis by the spring of my junior year, but we were both relieved the Dilantin was controlling her seizures. Together, we dared to take a college tour. Over spring break, we headed to North Carolina to visit three campuses I had interest in. Two of them attracted me with their beauty and course offerings. One also had a strong music program that I hoped Mom would find compelling. But in the end, no criteria carried enough weight to sway her from her choice for me.

"Why are you even thinking of going out of state? William and Mary is a fine school, and it's in-state."

*Here I am again, being forced onto your path.*

I was pissed off but resolved to keep the peace. She and Dad would be footing the bill after all. When I told her I wanted to apply to one of the "seven sister schools" in New England, she told me not to waste my money. My guidance counselor thought William and Mary was a long shot, even though I was in the top ten percent of my class. "You need to lower your expectations," she cautioned me.

The counselor had given me an out, though I did not realize it. Still, I had no interest in either of the schools she directed me to. She did not live with my mother nor understand I had no choice but to apply to her alma mater. Besides, I was now used to pushing back against the naysayers. I needed to prove the counselor wrong. So, I sent off my application for early admission to William and Mary and resolved to accept whatever fate might come. At least it made Mom happy.

The next week, I received notice that, as one of two junior women from my high school, I was chosen to attend Virginia Girls State, a week-long event sponsored by the American Legion. The goal of the immersion is to provide prospective leaders with an experiential lesson in self-governance from local to state levels. Young women from across Virginia gathered at Radford College, where we were divided into "cities" and assigned to one of two "political parties." Each city held local elections on our first day to choose mayors, city council members, city managers, etc. Somehow, I was the last one standing in Barrett City and was elected dog catcher. The thought of going home with that title was unbearable to me. Being a dog catcher is perfectly respectable, but I believed I was capable of being more. I lay on my bed in my dorm room and remembered my cuckoo clock.

*I'm going to run for governor.*

The next day, I filed to run, and after a three-day campaign, I defeated my worthy opponent. It spared me the humiliation of having to tell my father I was "just a dog catcher." I do not recall if a replacement was chosen to round up the mythical Barrett City canines.

# CHAPTER 18

Before Thanksgiving, a thick envelope arrived in my mailbox. My college acceptance letter was in hand. It was a gift that enabled me to enjoy the remainder of my senior year without having to worry about what came next after graduation. The route to my next destination was clear.

By the time spring was in full bloom, we all had senioritis. We were spiraling toward the end of the life I had come to love. My friends were receiving their college acceptances every day. We knew we would soon be torn apart, scattered by the winds, to create new lives without one another. My close-knit group of a dozen friends spent as much time together as we could. They were my safety net, and I was happy to have them to escape to when life at home was intolerable. We spent our Friday nights together in one another's homes, listening to Laura Nyro, Three Dog Night, and Blood, Sweat and Tears. I found escape from my war zone home in the music and presence of good friends.

We took a picnic lunch to Great Falls Park on senior skip day. We basked in the sun, reminisced, and shared our hopes for the future. A group of classmates showed up late—boys whose smell and stagger revealed their level of intoxication. We hiked up the cliffs overlooking the river. We stood high above the rapids on a bluff when Mike, one of the latecomers, picked me up and walked to the edge of the rocks with me in his arms and held me out over the water. There was a collective gasp from friends around us. I screamed but did not dare move. I froze, afraid he would lose his balance. The life flashing before me was one of a father who reeked of alcohol and staggered to the bathroom before falling into bed, and a mother who did not have the energy to care. I refused to believe this would be my ending. I closed my eyes and waited, my heart pounding in my throat. Somehow, someone pulled him back from the edge, and he put me down. I sank to the rocks below my feet, put my head in my hands and wept, while my friends surrounded me.

The following Friday, I hosted the music group at my house. As usual, we lounged in the living room, snacking on chips and drinking soda. Dad was drinking his "soda" in the den, and Mom was out of town. Around ten o'clock, my friends filed out the kitchen door one by one and headed home. When the last one left, and I closed the door, I turned to see Dad lurking behind me. His chin protruded, and his eyes focused on me like a laser. He was ready for another fight.

"I never want to see that Gary boy in this house again. Do you understand?"

He had not been this adamant for a while, but once again, his irrational anger was white-hot. I had no idea what Gary had done.

"No. I don't understand. What's wrong?"

"If he sets foot in this house again, I will kill him."

If Dad had a reason, he had either forgotten it or refused to reveal it. Instead of explaining, he glared at me, his eyes bulging, his cheeks puffed out. He looked like a crazy man. I knew better than to try to change his mind. But I was angry. Senior Prom was the following Saturday, and I had already sent invitations for a pre-dance dinner party. Gary was the class president; there was no way I would uninvite him. I had to find a workaround, but I had a lot going on. My peach-crepe prom dress awaited sleeves, and final exams were in two weeks. I needed to shop for and prepare food for the party. When I lamented my dilemma to a friend, she and a couple of others devised a plan.

The house was clean on Saturday, the table was set, and the food was ready. Mom was at a clinic in Florida, and Dad was gone; I had no idea where. I did not expect him to show up, but we had a plan in case he did. The guests arrived in their long gowns and tuxes and gathered in small groups, one in the living room, another in the kitchen, and the third in the carport. Every fifteen minutes or so, the groups moved from one location to another. On high alert, the group in the carport was on the lookout for Dad's green Chevy Nova to round the corner. The plan was: if they saw the car, they signaled the group in the kitchen, who alerted Gary. Gary was to rush downstairs and out the back door. I was relieved but not surprised: Dad never showed his face. Still, I wondered if he knew how he had ruined my night.

⁂

As Governor of Girls State, I was obligated to return the summer after my senior year to preside over the session until my successor was sworn in. But there was a complication. My graduation was the same week, and I had been selected to give the graduate speech. Missing either event was not an option, so I had to figure out how to be in two places at once. I had learned from our one great workaround for prom, so I was sure I could meet this challenge, too. Once again, my friends stepped up to help. I rode to Girls State with a delegate at the beginning of the week and flew into National Airport mid-week. A friend picked me up, bringing with her my white gown and gold-tasseled cap, and she dropped me off at school.

Rain caused the ceremony to be moved indoors from the football stadium. Mom and Dad found seats in the auditorium—not together. Gram and Gramps sat on bleachers in the gym, listening over the loudspeaker. My speech ended with the words of poet Lucy Larcom, "Whatever with the past has gone, the best is always yet to come." I believed her words with all my heart. I had to.

Diploma in hand, I went into the night to celebrate with friends. Early the next morning, Dad took me to the airport to return to Girls State. He took my suitcase from the trunk and walked into the terminal with me. Inside the door, he stopped and handed me my bag. He looked gaunt, almost ghostlike. He had lost weight, and his pants sagged. I was not sure what was left of him. There was sadness in his eyes as he pulled on his cigarette.

I did not have time or interest enough to be curious if he was all right. "Thanks," I said as I turned and sprinted away to catch my flight. I did not notice that I was trying to avoid being sucked into his vacuum of despair.

When the week was over, Linda, who had driven us to Radford the Sunday before, drove us back to Northern Virginia and dropped me off at a shopping center near home. Leo, the boy I had been dating for a few months, met me there. I tossed my bag into the back seat of his sleek red Mustang and climbed into the bucket seat next to him. I felt so happy, so carefree. I had graduated. I had served as Governor of Girls State. And I was proud I had maneuvered myself around the landmines along the way. I was riding high and looking forward to the next chapter. Leo pushed in his eight-track tape of Blood, Sweat and Tears, and we drove out of the parking lot listening to "You've Made Me So Very Happy."

My home, the brick ranch house with pea-green shutters, sat down in a bowl, surrounded by towering oak trees. Leo pulled his car onto the crest of the driveway and eased down the hill towards the carport when an indescribable feeling rushed through me. Or maybe it descended on me. Or it welled up from within me. Perhaps it was all three at once. The hair stood up on my arms, and a chill ran down my spine. Neither of us knew we had passed through an indiscernible curtain and moved from a crystal clear, warm June afternoon into a fog where it was impossible to see your hand in front of your face.

"Something's wrong," I said. It was an energy that wove itself around me like a cocoon.

Leo shifted the gears to park and turned off the engine. He looked over at me, but before he could utter a word in response, I jumped out of the car and ran across the carport and through the kitchen door. Leo trailed close behind. We found Mom sitting at the glass-topped table, holding a cup of tea. The house felt cold.

"Your father's dead." There was ice in her voice and no emotion on her face.

I had been hit with a baseball bat in the gut, but I was not sure if the shock was from the news or that I had had an inkling before walking in the door.

*Oh my God, did you kill him?*

"How? What happened?" I hoped she would say he stroked out or keeled over.

"The doctor says it was a heart attack."

I was suspicious.

"How did you know?" Leo glared at me as if he thought I had kept the news from him.

"I have no idea. I felt something." I brushed him off, annoyed that his interest was misplaced.

Months before, Dad had moved his bed into the bedroom between my room and the owner's suite.

Mom continued, sounding like she was reading a report from the morning newspaper on the table before her.

"He got out of bed in the middle of the night, collapsed up against the door, and died. I couldn't open the door. When the ambulance arrived, they had to climb a ladder and break the window to get to him."

By the time I arrived home, the room was clean. Too clean. All evidence erased. Evaporated in thin air. Even his car was gone. It was tempting to think they had agreed he would disappear. I might have pressed harder for a different version of the truth had it not been for the plywood nailed over the shattered window convincing me to believe her story.

*This doesn't add up.*

Mom was worried only about how to collect his belongings from his office. Otherwise, she had no words. There was no grief. No tears to mark the end of her twenty-year marriage. Her stoic demeanor left me at a loss. I was accustomed to taking my cues from those around me, so I was afraid to show any emotion at all.

*How am I supposed to feel? Where is the playbook? What are the rules for this part of the game?*

I might have grieved if I had known how or if I had thought I had permission to, but I did not. So, I opted for relief. Relief from the tantrums. Release from unrealistic or unarticulated expectations. Respite from the roller coaster ride. Reprieve from playing the pawn in their war games. No more wondering when he would come home or when the other shoe would drop. No more landmines to step on or triangles to wiggle out of.

There was no funeral, no memorial service. Mom refused to receive his ashes from the funeral home until the mortician convinced her she needed to take them for my sake.

"Mr. Greene made me bring home your father's ashes. I buried them under that rosebush at the top of the hill." She flicked her hand toward the bush outside the kitchen window, beyond the carport, making it clear she did not want to admit she had made such an effort. Her contempt, which once oozed quietly, now flowed freely. There was no love lost. They had been at war so long I did not even wonder when the marriage had died.

"OK." I did not know what else to say.

The relief that came at his death was accompanied by a feeling of cluelessness. I did not know how to talk to Mom about how I felt. I was unsure she cared, and I expected she would shut down any attempt I made to discuss it. I was inside a giant bubble, like the ones I had blown in the backyard on Golf Street as a kid. I was free-floating. Or was I free-falling?

*Is this what it feels like to be untethered?*

It took three days to get my bearings before I pulled out the new sewing machine Mom had let me keep. I lifted the blue case to the table and set it next to the pink swimsuit, awaiting spaghetti straps.

*I need to finish this to take to the beach next week.*

I unlatched the cover, and when I lifted it, a manilla envelope fell to the floor, its contents sliding onto the carpet. A dozen white number ten envelopes. Each one stamped. Each addressed in Dad's handwriting. None of the names were familiar. One by one, I slipped them back into the manilla envelope until one was left. It was addressed to me. I opened it and leaned on my bed as Mom walked by my room.

"Don't tell anyone about that note."

*What?*

I needed more from her, but I did not know what. A word? A signal? The truth would have been nice. But she had mastered the art of secret-keeping, and her behavior directed me to do the same. My eyes fell to the words on the paper that I held like a fragile flower—my hands trembling.

June 18, 1971

My Kitten:

Please forgive me for what I have done. Try to understand why I have taken my life. I told you about my failing health, but not about my job insecurity and the fact that I have no savings, or pension, or any other income to look forward to and, as you well know, a miserably unhappy life at home.

In the long run, financially, you and your Mother will be better off without me. There is enough insurance to keep your mother through a period of readjustment, and I have earmarked three insurance policies for you, so you will have enough to see you through college and still leave you some money, particularly if you get summer jobs, or teach piano. If you should run out of money (and make a note of this:) Get in touch with ▇▇▇▇▇▇▇ or ▇▇▇▇▇▇▇.

Keep your money in the bank, in a savings account. Don't invest it in stocks, or real estate, or anything else. And don't lend it to anybody, not even to your husband or to your best friend, unless you don't want to ever see your money again.

Outside of that, I have no advice to give you because you need no advice. Just continue the way you are going. You are doing great. You could do nothing better than you are doing right now. You use your head at all times, you are considerate, smart, humorous, talented, and cautious; also a bit of a politician. If you can be all these things now, at 17, what advice can I or anyone else give you?

Don't let my death affect your plans in any way. Just dry up your tears and say: "My Dad lived the way he wanted to, and he died when he wanted to, but he loved me very much."

Also, remember, Kitten, that nothing is everlasting.

Be sure, though, to complete your education so that you can earn a living later on.

It's too bad that you and I had so little communication. I suppose your mother's condition had a lot to do with it. I really got to know you rather recently, when your mother was in Florida and we had a chance to talk a little bit.

I do leave you another legacy: your star—the brightest star in the sky, which I gave you when you were about five years old. It's yours, all yours, and you can give it to your baby when she (or he) is five years old.

So, good-bye, my Kitten.

You have a long life ahead of you, but only one life, so enjoy it to the fullest extent. May it be a very happy life.

I love you very much.

Dad

Do me a few favors:

1. Insist that your mother follow my instructions: I don't want any funeral or any of that jazz. I just want to be cremated. Period.

2. Please make the phone calls indicated in the attached note and mail the letters right away. If you don't feel up to it, have someone else do it.

He had gone to great lengths. He intended to succeed. All those letters, addressed to his friends and colleagues, I suppose. And in mine—he had corrected every typo.

I wondered if he had left one for Mom, but I was not sure I wanted to know. It was too much to absorb. This was his parting shot, and I wilted inside like a flower without water. I wanted nothing to do with any of it, any of him. I sprinted to the blue mailbox on the corner up the street, shoved the letters down the chute, and wiped my hands on my shorts as though the envelopes had been laced with poison. For years, I needed to be rid of him.

Now, I was free. Or I tried to convince myself I was. In reality, a boiling rage bubbled beneath the shock and numbness.

*You selfish, selfish man. Good riddance.*

A few days later, I remembered seeing him standing in the airport the week before, holding a cigarette in one hand and waving goodbye to me with the other. And the blank expression on his face as though he was disappearing from the world at that very moment.

*What was he thinking? Did he know that would be my last memory of him?*

I tried to recall words we might have exchanged, but they were gone forever. All that remained was the vision of where he was standing when he said goodbye, alongside painful memories laced with the lingering odor of stale cigarette smoke and whiskey.

# CHAPTER 19

A grim cloud of grief descended and hung over me throughout the summer. Between Dad's death and the anticipated loss of my high school friends, I was at loose ends. But I was determined not to let it impact my next chapter. I prepared for my freshman year: packed my belongings and stuffed the empty spaces with equal measures of joy and anticipation. I planned to leave my grief behind. The trunk and backseat of Mom's white Ford Montego were filled with all that constituted my high school life, from clothes to stereo, hotpot to study pillow. We stood together in the kitchen, reviewing the checklist.

"We're all packed up. And besides, there's no more room. The car is full." I was eager to get on the road.

"There is one more thing," her voice was tentative.

I saw sadness in her face. Ten years of illness had taken its toll on her. I noticed it for the first time.

"What?"

"I need to tell you something."

*Oh geez. Here we go. What now?*

"I want you to know there is more to college than getting good grades."

*Oh. Did you notice I had made that my goal, that I busted my butt to get straight A's on my last report card?*

I did not know what to do with her words. And I wondered what the meaning was between them. Getting good grades was all that mattered to me up to that point. Competing against myself to do my best had driven me for so long. Be better. Do better. What could be more important? Was she releasing me from prison or pushing me from the nest? I filled in the blanks to suit myself.

*Grades no longer define me. I am free to make my own decisions and my own mistakes. There will be no one to threaten, shame, or save me.*

I wondered if she was bracing me for impact, to learn the lesson she had learned, that love is fleeting and a broken heart lasts a lifetime. When all those thoughts landed, it dawned on me that she would be left alone.

*Who will be here when she has another seizure? Who is going to take care of her? She has no job and not many friends to speak of. What is her life going to be?*

A shiver ran down my spine and I tried to settle the little girl in me who had sacrificed much to take care of her. I had cared for both of them long enough. I played my part in their drama and forfeited my childhood for them. It was time for me to write my own script. I buried my feelings and backed the car out of the driveway. I left home in the rearview mirror and assured myself she would be fine.

Our three-hour drive to campus ended when I pulled the car behind a chain of others in front of the DuPont residence hall. We moved the stuff of my life into my dorm room on the first floor of the east wing. When the last clothes were hung in the closet, Mom kissed me goodbye and headed home. I turned into a ball of manic energy. My roommate from Indiana had a calm demeanor, quite a contrast to my agitation. She realized sooner than I did that we were opposite from one another in almost every way. She was an athlete; I was a partier. She was an academic ace; I struggled for every A I got. She kept her feet planted on solid ground; I bounced around. We managed to get along.

I looked to others to help heal my pain, unaware I was replicating a pattern I had grown up with. I sought new adventures as a way to bury my grief, but I did it in all the wrong places and all the wrong ways. I would have been better off focusing on my grades, but I hopped on a train to self-destruct instead. Fraternity parties, drunken weekends, missed curfews. If I was not hungover on Sunday morning, I went to church, but the hour echoed with empty promises and gave me no peace. God was distant at best, irrelevant at worst, and most of all, unwilling to fill the hole left by Dad's death. Lacking academic incentives, I became an uninspired student overnight. The thought of arriving late to class was humiliating, so if I overslept, I skipped class altogether. I managed to keep my grades high enough not to flunk out, but I knew I was struggling. In fact, I was bleeding—all over the place. I was sure no one else noticed, much less cared.

Toward the end of the fall semester, a classmate who had made the freshmen cheerleading squad with me and whom I first met at Girls State invited me to walk to the corner deli with her.

She was a beauty queen with a thick Southern accent and a killer smile. She was a magnet. Everyone loved her, including me, but I was out of her league. I did not have the class or the allure she did. I did not feel the need to, but when she invited me to go for a soda with her, I jumped at the chance.

We sat in a booth with green vinyl cushions and a yellow table—school colors. The walls were filled with pictures of college athletes from the past. The football players in the photos seemed to lean in as if they intended to eavesdrop on our conversation about sorority rush. When our sodas arrived, she changed the subject.

"I am worried about you."

She had been at those frat parties and seen my poor choices and erratic behavior. She fretted for my future. I was shocked. No one had ever expressed such authentic care for me. No manipulation. No judgment. No shaming. No humiliation. No advice. Just care.

Her words were a warm blanket around me, with a cup of hot chocolate and a teddy bear to boot. At first, I was not sure what to do with her words—they sounded like a foreign language. But, in time they motivated me. They freed me from my path to self-destruction. I came up for air. I gave up drinking and started to focus on my studies.

When I returned to my dorm room after class on the December 10, I found a bouquet of white roses on the hallway floor in front of my door. There was no note attached, but I knew who they were from. It was the tenth anniversary of my first piano lesson. Mom set me free. No words were ever spoken.

Her gift of liberation proved to be both a blessing and a curse. I was relieved knowing I would never give another piano performance. But it was also uncomfortable not knowing where to turn; I had to change my major. When I registered for spring classes, I peppered my course list, hoping to find a subject to be passionate about. Spanish literature? I had a good grasp of the language. Sociology? I was curious about humans. Geology? The guy I was spending time with said it was easy. I was in the midst of an existential crisis, but I knew I would figure it out. I always did. I wandered for three semesters in an academic wasteland of my own making before settling on a major: geology.

By the fall of my junior year, life had a comfortable rhythm. I had joined a sorority and made the varsity cheerleading squad. My insecurities had faded—somewhat. Roots secured me to the earth. I felt grounded again. Fall break was coming up, and it seemed like a perfect time to drive to the Shore. I decided to pay a surprise visit to Gram and Gramps.

I threw my overnight bag into the passenger seat of my lemon-yellow Ford Pinto, the car Dad had given me as a graduation gift. It was a brilliant October day. There was not a cloud in the sky. Golden yellow, cherry red, and rusty orange leaves on the trees waved to me as I traveled eastward. I turned north on Route 13, toward the seventeen-mile span of bridges and tunnels crossing the Chesapeake Bay. My spirits were high as I took in the magnificent expanse of water with boats bobbling on the waves and seagulls diving into the whitecaps. Nostalgia swept over me as I recalled the days we took the ferry across these waters for a day of shopping. I missed the boat ride, but this was more expedient.

The wheels hit the solid ground of the Shore, and I rolled down the window and invited the clean salt air that tingled my nose into my lungs. The breeze carried the message of the farm calling my name. I was going home, and contentment filled me like a warm cup of Earl Grey tea on a crisp fall morning. But when I knocked on the door, Gram's countenance made it clear she did not share my delight. Her familiar ear-to-ear grin was replaced with a scowl.

"You should have called first." Her voice was cold.

*I'm glad to see you too. Why did I bother?*

Joy sucked out of me like air out of a pierced balloon. She held the screen door for me but did not offer me food or drink. That was the second clue that something was amiss. I could not recall a time when her first words were not, "What can I get you to drink?" or "You must be hungry after such a long trip." Almost always, she greeted me with a jar full of candy, a bowl of fresh picked figs, or a plate of blonde brownies. Not this time. Instead, she blew her whistle to beckon Gramps from the barn. He arrived in minutes, ducked into the powder room to wash his hands, and joined us in the den. We sat together exchanging pleasantries about the weather, gossip about their neighbors who lived further down the lane, and news about their friends at church. They politely inquired about school, and after a long pause, Gram said,

"Lolly's seizures are coming more often."

That was when I noticed the worry lines etched deep into her face.

Gramps sat silent for several minutes, tapping his fingers on the arms of his chair before suggesting, "You should have gone home to see her."

*You're retired. You should go to see her.*

My jaw clenched. As I tried to think of what to say, I recalled a story Mom had told me a few years earlier: when Aunt Mary died, Gram and Gramps withheld the news from Mom, not wanting to upset her because she was so ill. Their decision hurt Mom and robbed her of the opportunity to attend the funeral, stealing from her any chance to grieve. My playmate died that day, too, but that was of no importance to Gram. Her unilateral choice left both of us to sift through our memories alone.

*The news of Mary's death blindsided us. Are they trying to do better now?*

They stared at me with heavy expectation. They would not tell me what to do, but their faces said it all.

*I am so tired of taking care of everyone else.*

In the morning, I packed up and drove home to spend twenty-four hours with Mom. She told me about her recent visit to a prestigious Maryland hospital where yet another doctor put her through the same battery of tests that she had already endured multiple times. He told her the tests were inconclusive and that she needed to find a psychiatrist.

*I see why Gram and Gramps sent me home—to hear this directly from her.*

I wondered if Mom had told them the last part. Anyone who had seen her seize knew this was not a psychiatric condition. The doctor was full of crap. Mom knew it, and so did I. His words must have poured frustration on top of her anger. An oil barrel and a match.

A few months later, after the Christmas holiday, she had an appointment with a local neurologist who saw the problem. "You have a brain tumor," he told her, shocked that no one else had found it.

# CHAPTER 20

## When Worlds Collide

Plate tectonics is a geological theory that the earth's outer shell, the lithosphere, is comprised of several large plates. Scientists posit that these plates float on a liquid outer crust, and they move around, similar to a raft on the surface of a lake. The boundaries between plates are called faults. They are defined by their motion, of which three types exist.

A transform boundary results in the plates rubbing against one another horizontally. It happens most often on the ocean floor and is often linked to other types of plate movement. California's San Andreas Fault is a transform boundary on a continental margin. Driving from Los Angeles to San Diego along Route 1, the disrupted pavement displays clear evidence of the creeping damage that has been done to the earth's surface. Earth grinding against itself, back and forth. A masticating monster.

A divergent boundary occurs when two plates move away from one another, and the earth splits wide open. The movement causes rifts, which are transformed into valleys. Divergent boundaries occur most often in the ocean, but mi abuela told a story of this happening on land when she was a child—the ground separated beneath people's feet and thousands of innocents fell into the abyss.

A convergent boundary forms when two plates collide, and one slips under the other. These impacts generate the most severe earthquakes and volcanoes, creating magnificent mountain ranges. The Himalayas and the Southern Alps of New Zealand exemplify the potential beauty that can result from such collisions. The Pacific Ring of Fire is a tectonic belt filled with these boundaries, approximately 25,000 miles long, extending northward from the southwestern tip of South America to Alaska and southward across the western coastline of the Pacific Ocean.

When plates meet, worlds collide, the earth shakes, trenches form, and volcanoes erupt, forever altering the landscape.

# CHAPTER 21

The extended family was relieved to hear the doctor's diagnosis, but as the date of Mom's surgery approached, dark foreboding clouds gathered over us. Given the long, harrowing journey she had endured for almost fifteen years, we wanted to anticipate the best outcome but were hesitant to be too hopeful, lest our optimism be dashed.

I requested excused absences from my classes and extensions on assignments and drove home from school. It was the spring of my junior year, and I only wanted to maintain my momentum toward an on-time graduation the following year. Well, that and a quick surgery and recovery for Mom, of course. Dick, Mom's brother, flew in from California. It was a gift I was grateful for: not to have to navigate this treacherous terrain alone.

Brain surgery in 1974 was far more advanced than in 1884 when British surgeon Rickman Godley removed the first neurological tumor. Mom's surgery was not considered exploratory, but that did not mean the doctor could give us assurances. The words of the neurosurgeon tempered our positivity.

"We don't know what we will find when we get in there," the doctor said to us before the orderly rolled her bed from the room and down the long, cold corridor.

I was too naïve and timid to push the doctor to explain why it was a good idea to cut into Mom's head without knowing what they were going in for. Instead, I trusted the experts and followed the plan without raising questions.

With Mom on her way to surgery, Dick and I took the elevator to the ground-floor cafeteria. We bought bagels and coffee to take to the lobby, the waiting room for the families of surgical patients. We walked scores of laps around the hospital halls for an exhausting eight hours. When the doctor appeared, he was still wearing his green scrubs and cap, his blue mask pulled down to his chin. He directed us to a nearby consultation room. It was stark, sterile, and as cold as a freezer, apparently intended for brief conversations—no one would want to hang out there for long.

"We cut away part of her skull and were able to remove a tumor the size of a small grapefruit." He was professional in his detail.

"It is cancer. I can't be certain we got it all. We will determine follow-up treatment in the coming weeks. The skull bone has been replaced with a metal plate to protect her brain. She is in recovery now. When she is moved to the ICU, the nurse will call you, and you can see her."

*A grapefruit-sized mass? In her head?*

I imagined the skull of the Halloween skeleton in the yard next door. A skull with a hole the size of a softball. None of what he said sounded good to me. I could not read between the lines of his message delivered without encouragement. I did not dare imagine what the future held nor press him for a vision for her future, afraid that he would smash my threads of hope that were as sheer as a spider's web.

An hour later, we tiptoed into the ICU and stood at the doorway to her room. A shudder shook me.

*Is it my anxiety or is it freezing in here?*

Mom's room smelled antiseptic, and the sounds from beeping machines and hissing oxygen bounced off the walls. Wires and tubes connected her to all the noise.

A nurse looked up when she heard our footsteps. "This machine—we call it a brain—monitors her vitals and rations her drugs."

*A brain? Isn't that ironic?*

She finished checking the lines running into Mom's arms. "I'll leave you to visit. Here is the call button if you need me."

Mom awoke in a fog, very much under the influence of anesthesia. Her head was wrapped in bandages. She mustered a smile when she saw us. "That wasn't so bad," she mumbled in a calm voice, as though she had just finished an easy exam.

She closed her eyes and dozed off. We left her to sleep. The stress of pacing and waiting had exhausted us, so we went home to tend to our own recovery.

The clock on the wall chimed seven the next morning. I sat at the kitchen table, eating a piece of toast and drinking a cup of coffee. Dick was in the shower. I jumped when the phone rang. It was too early for a call.

"Hello?"

"Janice?"

"Yes?"

"This is Kathy in the ICU at Fairfax Hospital. Overnight, your mother's brain swelled. The edema is putting pressure on her brain. The doctor needs to take her into surgery to remove the plate and relieve the pressure. He is prepping for surgery now. It is a simple procedure and won't take long."

"Oh. Okay. Thank you. We will be there as soon as we can. Thank you."

I hung up the phone and sank back into my chair. The doctor had not prepared us for a setback this soon. Dick and I pulled ourselves together and rushed to the hospital to wait for an update. Within an hour, the doctor informed us the metal plate had been removed without causing damage.

"The edema is subsiding. Without the plate, her brain has room to breathe. Her recovery should be fast now."

We were relieved and waited until she was moved back to the ICU. As it turned out, our relief was premature. The doctor had taken quick action, but not fast enough. Following the surgery, Mom lapsed into a coma. If the day before had been the ride up the roller coaster hill, this was the day our hopes dropped fast and steep, spinning us in a loop before coming to a hard stop.

We prayed. The doctor was tentative in his encouragement, but we maintained confidence that she would wake up with a smile at any moment. But the days turned into weeks, and our hope became overshadowed by doubts, "what ifs," and worst-case scenarios.

Dick saw there was little more he could do to be helpful, so he booked his flight back to California. It was the end of April, and my exams were coming up. I needed to get back to school, but Gram and Gramps made clear their expectation that I stay home and visit Mom all day every day. I did not know what they thought that would accomplish. They said they would come from the Shore in a week to relieve me so I could return to Williamsburg and finish the semester. I phoned my professors and arranged for my boyfriend to collect lecture notes and assignments and bring them to me on the weekend, so I would have what I needed to prepare for my exams.

Gram and Gramps called every evening for updates on Mom's condition.

"There's been no change," I reported to them on Thursday.

"I'm sorry to hear that," Gram said.

"Yes." I paused. "You know, my exams start in two weeks. Ben is coming tomorrow, bringing me the notes and assignments I need to prepare for the end of the semester."

Silence. A long silence. I thought the phone had gone dead. I did not know whether to speak or hang up. I was about to open my mouth when

Gram said, "Don't do anything God wouldn't approve of, or He won't heal your mother."

Words left me. Feelings abandoned me, leaving only numbness.

*What do I say to that?*

Blood rushed to my face, and my jaw clenched. Tears filled my eyes, but I was too hurt, insulted, and angry to cry.

*What does she think of me?*

Now, the silence was on my end. It was long. And dark. I wanted to scream, but I did not dare.

*Should I hang up?*

"Yeah. Okay. I have to go." I slammed the receiver down.

*What kind of God would punish Mom for something I did? I can't believe in that God. I need to figure out if there is a god I can believe in.*

The room around me disappeared. I stood, frozen, in the kitchen for a long time, staring out the window at the rose bush where Mom had stashed Dad's ashes. He was gone. She was inaccessible. The doting grandmother I once adored was now a stranger to me. And without warning, God was a foreign concept I did not dare entertain. I was alone. By the time Ben arrived, I was enveloped in a void of impenetrable loneliness and haunted by Gram's words.

Gram and Gramps arrived on Monday afternoon. We visited Mom in the ICU, where the doctor gave us what little news he could: the pathology report.

"She will need radiation and chemotherapy. At best, she may have ten more years. But we don't want to start a regimen until she comes out of the coma. So, we wait."

Looking at me, he said, "Go back to school. Finish your semester. This is going to take time."

I heeded the doctor's orders and returned to school the next day. I clawed my way to class each day, existing from one assignment to the next. This was familiar territory. I had been here before: unable to focus, swallowed by an invisible monster. Kind professors gave me extensions to complete my coursework, removing the pressure I tried to put on myself. Sorority sisters applauded my return. Ben's fraternity brothers sheltered me as if I were a younger sister. Surrounded by good people who meant well, I eked out passing grades and finished the semester.

Mom was still in a coma when I got home for the summer. She showed no signs of improvement. No smile. No response to my voice. But the nurses encouraged me to talk to her.

"You never know—she might hear you."

One afternoon, Mrs. Rose, the hospital social worker, strolled tentatively into Mom's room. "The insurance company will no longer cover her hospital expenses. She needs to be moved to a nursing facility for further care. Here's a list of places for you to consider."

She put a pile of papers on the table, leaflets of nearby nursing homes, and cheat sheets on what we could expect and what questions we should ask. She left the room oblivious to the disorder she left behind. My heart dropped to the floor like a stone. Tears filled Gram's eyes, a saltwater fountain ready to explode. Gramps' chin sunk to his chest. He had fought in World War I. Exploding rockets were no surprise to him, but he never saw this bombshell coming.

Gram and Gramps decided to move into my home for the summer and stay into the fall so I could complete my senior year. They presented their plan to me like a framed picture they assumed I wanted. They were committed to me finishing school. Gram believed someone had to spend every day at Lolly's bedside. There was no fault in her wanting to do that. But she also sent frequent and not-so-subtle reminders that they were sacrificing for me. If that was not enough, she anointed herself as my mother's surrogate, monitoring my every move. She expected I would be at the nursing home when I was not working.

The stress of waiting for Mom to emerge from the cocoon in her brain made everyone's patience work harder than the air conditioner. It was a summer of record heat as the days turned to weeks, and my independence melted like tar on a hot summer day.

Ben returned for a visit over his birthday weekend in July. I prepared his favorite birthday cake—Toffee Angel Food. After hollowing out the angel food to make room for the whipped cream, I put the remnants on a plate and invited Gram and Gramps to help themselves.

"Don't be so rude," she scolded. "You should give me a whole piece of cake."

*It's Ben's birthday! He gets the first piece.*

Her entitlement stung me. But that was only the beginning. As the summer wore on, she became more judgmental and restrictive.

I had a summer internship at Quantico Marine Base, using my geology knowledge to support the Army's war games. One evening after work, a soldier invited me to dinner. Gram wanted to know more about him. When I told her he was divorced, she unleashed a tirade of judgments.

"Your life will always be one of compromise." She pronounced her bottom line.

*That is one giant leap. It is none of your business. And I'm curious: Did you say that to Mom before she married Dad?*

Gram did not stop there. I understood the stress and pain she was under, but she leveled new and unwarranted grievances at me each day. I let most of them slide; I had no energy to push back until, one day, out of the blue, she sliced through me with a sharp razor's edge.

"Your mother wanted to go with you to Florida last spring. She was shattered that you didn't take her with you."

*Are you serious? Moms do not go to Daytona Beach with their daughters on spring break.*

I was done. I no longer wanted to be under the same roof with her. But once again, I was expected to play the role of the compliant child. Her word was the law, and I had to live by it. Gram's boundaries that had blurred with Mom's were encroaching on mine. The complaints she laid at my feet sharpened my insecurities and re-established my self-doubt. My shame skyrocketed while my self-esteem crashed. I was in a vice between Gram's expectations and Mom's never-ending recovery.

As the summer dragged on, my visits to the hospital grew shorter and shorter. I could not bear to see her in this vegetative, non-communicative state. My hope flailed while Gram and Gramps held a daily vigil at Mom's bedside all summer. They carried their rose-colored faith to the nursing home in a basket filled with gospel passages and divine promises. Gram sang hymns. Gramps exercised her arms, legs, and hands. They were drawn-out days punctuated by occasional glimpses of hope. The blink of an eye. The movement of her lips. The uttering of the number seven several times. We allowed each one to fan the fading embers of our yearning, but no sooner did we dare to believe the sheath was dissolving than another seizure sent her back to the hospital. A week later, she returned by ambulance to her dull, gray room at the nursing home. There, she spent her days in a wheelchair, strapped in to keep her limp body from sliding to the floor, her head held in place by a pillow, her face ashen and expressionless. By the time I returned to campus in late August, my dreams for her full recovery had evaporated into a hollow aspiration.

# CHAPTER 22

Gram and Gramps were ensconced in my home as I returned to campus for my senior year. They missed their farm, but they had cultivated a new routine. My priority was to get through the year and graduate. I wanted to experience what my classmates enjoyed—light, joyful revelry. They prepared for their next chapters and relegated memories to the pages of photo albums. They chose color schemes for their weddings. They accepted job offers or invitations to graduate programs. Happy futures were on their horizon, but I could not dare imagine the days ahead, much less the months. The heavy burden that weighed me down may as well have been an anchor pulling me to the bottom of the Creek.

Mom's failure to escape the dark tunnel of her brain and my skepticism about her recovery infiltrated the hole where I had felt safe for so long. I did not dare let anyone in on my reality for fear I would damper their elation. I held my chin up, tucked away my apprehensions, and crept through the dark one step at a time. I managed passing grades and went home on weekends when time allowed. It was a split-life existence—my body at school, my mind at home, my soul in limbo.

Attempting to cope, to understand it all, to find peace if not an answer, I searched for God, though I still was not sure who God was. I explored religious expressions beyond my own, but they offered little that was more meaningful than what I already had in my own United Methodist roots. The Presbyterian, Baptist, and Episcopalian preachers all spoke of a God I could not relate to. He seemed formulaic and distant, prescribed and remote. So, I picked up my Bible and tried to make sense of it on my own. Each morning, I climbed down from my top bunk on the third floor of the sorority house, slipped on my robe, picked up my Bible and journal, and tiptoed out onto the landing. I sat in the rocking chair, Bible in my lap, bargaining with God.

*If you heal Mom, I will give my life to you.*

Depression and desperation became constant companions. The world made no sense. None of the pieces of my life fit together. Mom was right. There was more to college than grades. But her words had not prepared me for this. My future was a geology degree. Beyond that, my path was unknown. It took all of my emotional energy to complete assignments and get to class. Looking for a job was an unreasonable expectation I could not place on myself. Besides, I had no interest in pursuing a career in geology, and the thought of a music job lay in the trash alongside the roses Mom had sent to set me free.

Graduation day arrived. Gram, Gramps, and Mom's cousins came to town to represent my absent parents and to bear witness to my survival. With my diploma in hand and tassel turned, I sat alone on the front porch of the sorority house and took a moment to let the reality sink in.

*I made it.*

We celebrated that day. It was, by all measures, a true accomplishment worthy of pride and merriment. Smiles, hugs, and shouts of joy filled Sorority Court. Then, one by one, the sisters emptied their rooms. They poured out of their houses in giddy streams of bliss. Their cars packed to the gills with their belongings, their hearts sealed with memories. My Pinto was packed, too, and it was time to go. But as the hatchback closed, I watched the curtain come down on my closing night. The stage of what was supposed to have been the best years of my life was going dark forever. My glory days had been compromised. I stood on the stage alone now. The lights dimmed. The audience gone. The heroine bearing the weight of a tragic ending. Like her, I too, was dying.

I drove the lonely highway home, wiping tears along the way. Once my car was unpacked and I was settled in back at home, I went to see Mom. She had suffered another seizure in the nursing home and was back in the hospital, tracked by wires and fed through tubes. Monitors beeped. The oxygen concentrator gurgled. A gauze-wrapped tongue depressor for use in case of another seizure was taped to the wall over her bed. The hall was filled with the sounds of whispering nurses and scurrying orderlies. I sat at her bedside, my tears spilling out onto her bedsheets. I took her bony cold hand into mine.

"Mom, I did it. I finished. I graduated."

Noises in the hallway faded into the background as I felt her hand give mine a weak but discernible squeeze. She knew. Did she feel anything? Relief? Pride? Gratitude? I could not know, but I knew she heard me. For a split second, contentment filled me, and warmth wrapped around me. With all the uncertainty ahead of us, I prayed this news made her happy. If she shared my joy for this one moment, it was enough.

By the end of the week, Gram and Gramps were packed and ready to return to the farm, leaving me alone to figure out… well, everything. They were eager to return to their little piece of heaven, but not without leaving me with clear expectations.

"You will visit her every day, won't you?"

*That's not really a question, is it?*

"You won't do anything God wouldn't approve of."

*That was definitely not a question.*

That was all she said. Not even words of encouragement to find a job. Gram expected me to take her place. To sit at Mom's bedside all day, every day. To pick up where she left off. To coax Mom back to consciousness. Her persistent vegetative state did not present us with a decision to discontinue life support. She was not on a respirator. We were all in limbo, but even the doctors and nurses urged me to get on with my life.

*We all did our part, what was expected of us. They went beyond the call, sacrificing fourteen months on the farm for me. I should be grateful.*

The truth was I could not muster a speck of gratitude. I appreciated their sacrifice, but the anger and betrayal I harbored towards Gram, alongside the creeping sense of abandonment, caused me to retreat to the safety of my emotional hole. I could not bear to spend every day at Mom's side. She was not there anymore. A tube in her nose where the orderly pushed brown sustenance of some sort. A catheter to drain her bladder to confirm she was receiving and eliminating enough fluids. Another little part of her seemed to fade away each time I visited. She was speechless, and I was forgetting the sound of her voice. The thought of never hearing her speak again smashed through me like a wrecking ball, leaving me flat on the nursing room floor.

Her doctors and nurses saw where this was headed. Their eyes conveyed regret for what was to come. I could not bring myself to ask them for a prognosis, and they dropped no hints, but the looks on their faces and the message between their unspoken lines said it all. She was not going home. She was not going to recover.

I needed to find a job. The money from Dad's insurance policy was not going to last forever. Spending all day at the hospital was taking a toll on my already fragile mental health. I answered a couple of want ads and ended up working as a file clerk with the State Water Control Board. It was neither exciting nor well-paying, but I needed to stay busy and distracted enough to fend off pangs of guilt for not picking up where Gram left off at Mom's side.

I met a friend for dinner after work on September 3. We had "wonderful beef" at a Chinese restaurant and laughed ourselves silly, trying to figure out what made it wonderful. Within five minutes of arriving home, my enjoyment of the evening was smashed by a knock on the kitchen door. Ellen, our neighbor across the street and alternative emergency contact for the nursing home, stood in the carport looking through the screen. Her face delivered the message. Her words evaporated in the air before finding my ears. All I heard her say was,

"Gref is coming to take you to the nursing home."

Gref was a high school friend who attended Ellen's church. I invited Ellen in, and she stayed with me until he arrived. But I was already shutting down, enveloped in a bubble that protected me from all my emotions. Mom was gone. I was numb. Three weeks short of my twenty-second birthday, I was an orphan.

When he arrived, Ellen walked me to his car and opened the door for me.

"Thank you," I whispered as I climbed in.

She closed the door and held her hand up as if to bless us as we backed out of the driveway.

Mom's ashen and lifeless body lay in the bed. Her short, wiry gray hair covered the sinkhole on the left side of her skull where they had extracted the grapefruit. There was no peace on her face. She was gone. I was crushed. But as before, I had no script.

*What do I do? What am I supposed to do? I cannot stand here. I can't stand the pain.*

Guilt, shame, abandonment, grief, desperation, and desolation paralyzed me all at once, but fear was the leech that latched onto me and won out.

"Do I have to stay here?" my voice wafted over the bed to the night shift nurse.

"No. You don't have to stay. We will take care of things."

I grabbed the bag filled with her belongings from the end of her bed and walked out as fast as I could without running.

*Can I outrun the pain?*

Gref was waiting for me in his car parked in front of the nursing home. When I opened the door, he twisted the key in the ignition and put the car in drive. We were not out of the parking lot before I heard Helen Reddy's voice, her words a scalpel slicing through my heart. "When one of us is gone… remembering…memories… I love you, Mommy." My sobs drowned out her words.

*What will I do without my Mom?*

We had our conflicts, to be sure, but I was not prepared to let her go. My love for her and my angst of being alone fed the darkness surrounding me. By the time Gref dropped me back at home, my world was black. I was going through the motions without emotions, all of my feelings stashed in a garbage bag.

I roamed the house, moving from room to room in slow motion—a human lava lamp. The furniture was all there, but the place was empty. Standing in the kitchen, I remembered Mom's first seizure. I walked past the dining room and recalled prom night—the table filled with food, our laughter and revelry. I paused at the piano in the living room long enough to shake my head. I looked down the stairs to the basement, where Dad's paintings hung askew on the walls, and the smell of his stale cigarette smoke still haunted me. I walked to the bedrooms. The one in the middle where Dad died. Mom's room in the back of the house, her closets filled with yellow suits, brown slacks, and beige dresses.

I paced in an endless loop, wanting to wake from this bad dream. At last, unable to stand any longer, I sat and sank like a stone into the rust-colored sofa that had replaced the bed in the room where Dad died. Reality closed in on me. I lived among the dead—surrounded by ghosts. The glow from the light on the table was my only assurance the world had not come to an end. But I was not sure I could trust the light to keep burning.

At last, I moved to my bedroom, where I stood for a long time, looking out the window, begging the trees to make me believe there was a life ahead of me. The light from the streetlamp shimmered on the cinnamon and paprika-tinged leaves, hinting at the season's oncoming change. They held onto their source as if to assure me life was still good, but it struck me as bragging. Then, an unexpected breeze whooshed, and one leaf levitated off its branch. It floated away, riding the current, a spirit raised by an angel. The still green leaf took its leave prematurely, just as Mom had. I stepped closer to the window to follow its trajectory, but it was gone, whisked away into eternity. To gather with others. To dwell in a realm unseen.

🐚

None of the adults ever wanted a big to-do at death. We never talked about fancy funerals or bought burial plots. No one dreamed of an expensive casket or large sprays of flowers. Mom was no exception. Gram and Gramps drove from the Shore. Dick and Helen flew in from California. A small group of family and friends gathered in a neighborhood church, where a picture of a young Mom sat on the altar. Sun on her face. Wind in her hair. Ocean in the background. She was happy.

The following day, Gram and Gramps packed up their black Chrysler to return to the farm, taking Mom's ashes with them. I stood in the driveway watching their car fade into the distance. That was the moment I recalled a dinner conversation at the farm many years earlier—I might have been eleven or twelve. It was a warm evening, with a cool breeze sweeping off the Creek. Gram, Gramps, Mom, and I had been fishing in the afternoon, and we were at the dining room table finishing our dinner of sautéed trout, cornbread, sliced tomatoes, and snap beans.

"When I die," Mom said, "I want to scatter my ashes in the Chesapeake Bay."

I giggled, trying to imagine how she planned to pull it off, but neither Gram nor Gramps saw its humor. The way it turned out, I wondered if they had even heard her.

Gram purchased a Revere Ware stock pot with a copper bottom. She took the urn filled with Mom's ashes, meticulously wrapped it in a thick layer of newspaper, placed it in several clear plastic bags, and tightly bound it with DuckTape. Gramps dug a hole in her garden outside the den window. She placed the urn in the stockpot and lowered it into the hole. It was as close as she could get to letting go of her Lolly. She pulled the weeds from the garden and planted white phlox around a plaque Gramps had ordered. It read,

LAURA CHOATE QUINN

LOLLY

OCT 10, 1923–SEPT 3, 1975

Six weeks later, I resigned from my job. I could not sit still. Restlessness was the washing machine agitating my psyche. I wanted to run away from death. So, I flew to California to visit Dick and Helen. But as the holidays approached, I sensed reality catching up with me. I wanted to avoid life and stay in sunny southern California, but a sense of duty pulled me to the farm to be with Gram and Gramps on Christmas. I flew home on Christmas Eve and drove straight to the Shore. We had no Christmas tree. There were no decorations or gifts. In their place was a heavy obligation and a mantle of sadness.

# CHAPTER 23

After the holidays, I went back to Reston to look for another job. Though I did not intend to use my geology degree after graduation, it satisfied the requirements for a position as cartographer at the US Geological Survey. I spent each day sitting on a stool, peering over a light table in a dark room surrounded by odd fellows. Two creepy men in our lab hid their misogyny poorly. Another kept to himself while he consumed Pepsi by the liter and potato chips by the party-sized bag and muttered derogatory remarks at everyone who walked by. Cindy was friendly but cagey and took a lot of cigarette breaks. Leona, our "mother superior," brought us assignments, instructed us with firm words, and chastened us to approach our work with extreme care.

Map-making is tedious and exacting work. It requires patience and skill to work with layer upon layer of mylar film, each a different color, every color signifying a distinct rock formation. Straight edges and etchers are used to draw the lines with precision. There is no room for error or a slip of the hand. Within six months, I had an inkling that this was not what I was supposed to be doing. I needed to be crafting a map of my own life. I was alone in the world and in charge of my destiny. But what did it mean? Mom was not going to tell me what to do now.

*Who am I? Who do I want to become?*

The questions tore open the unhealed wound that was the loss of my parents, and my panging for them pounded harder than my heart. No one was there to coach me. Mom was not there to push me where she thought I should go. I was shaken from my sadness by the realization that, perhaps, I was better off. I could chart my course my way.

*Cue Frank Sinatra.*

I still had a bone to pick with God and sought out a large church where I thought I could do that. I dove in, joining the choir and gathering a group of young adults for Bible study. I needed to know more about God, the Bible, the church. I needed to figure out if God was nudging me towards something, or if I was running from something else. A hunger drilled deep into my soul and pushed me to seminary. I prepared to start classes in Washington, DC, in September, two years after Mom's death.

🙦

Weeks before the semester began, Gramps stood on the sidewalk in Exmore, waiting to cross the street to pick up a gasket at The Western Auto Store. Gram sat in the car and watched as he stepped into the street in front of a vehicle that slammed into him and sent him flying. Despite the rush by ambulance to the nearest trauma hospital ninety minutes away, he succumbed to his internal injuries that evening.

The vitality of "heaven on earth" was sucked away that day, as though a tornado had come through and wiped it off the map. The farm assumed a shroud-like quality, a gray shawl draped over the land no number of memories or beautiful surroundings could lift. Dick, Helen, and I descended on the farm as fast as we could get there. Gram wore her grief deeply. Her smile disappeared, as did her laugh. She wished aloud it had been her instead of Gramps, who had been taken in an instant. She could not bring herself to cook or eat. She spoke in soft and heavy tones. She walked alone to the dock and stood for hours as if waiting for Gramps to pull up in the boat and take her away with him.

There was no memorial service. A simple, lonely lowering of his urn into the ground, an urn preserved and protected in the same way Lolly's had been. When the hole was filled, and the soil was smoothed over, Gram covered it with a plaque that read,

HERMAN MICHAEL QUINN

US ARMY

WORLD WAR I

AUG 28, 1891–AUG 11, 1977

We each grieved separately. Helen cooked while Gram walked alone around her rose garden. Dick sat in Gramps' brown easy chair with his glass of gin. I watched Gram from the den window, and my gaze turned to the locust tree by the cove. I remembered the story of his refusal to leave the farm during Hurricane Donna. Mom tried to persuade them to evacuate, but Gramps would not, and Gram would not go without him. He tethered the boat to that locust tree. The tide rose, and the wind whipped up. The rope came loose, and Gramps swam out to grab and refasten it to the tree. He saved the boat. His cherished stamp collection in the trunk in barn three did not fare so well—stamps floated atop the receding waters while in barn one, a jellyfish pulsed in the front seat of the water-logged Chrysler.

I strolled down my own memory lane. Gramps loved Malabar pepper and ground it fresh on every meal. He relished stinky cheese, Manhattans, and dark Lowenbrau beer. The rasping sound as he sharpened his antler-handled knife to carve the Thanksgiving turkey echoed in my head. He piled all his food in the middle of his plate. There was no separating meat from vegetables from starch.

"It all goes to the same place," he said when I wrinkled my nose.

He was wedded to his routines. Arising at six in the morning, he dressed and crept down the stairs to the kitchen to prepare coffee for Gram when she came down at eight. While the coffee perked, he took a shot glass from the pantry shelf, cracked a raw egg into it, poured an ounce of sherry over it, and swallowed it in one gulp. Every weekday at five p.m., he turned on his radio to get the stock market report, picked up his mechanical pencil, and jotted down the closing Dow Jones Industrial Average on his calendar. He tracked hurricanes with similar diligence, pulling out maps of the Caribbean Sea or the Atlantic Ocean and marking the progress of storms lest one develop with the potential to impact the farm.

His smile and gentle demeanor defined him. He deferred to Gram most of the time. He collected cereal box tops and traded them in for rose bushes for Gram's garden. He loved the water, sailing, fishing, and me. And I loved him—very much.

A month after we buried Gramps, I started seminary. I took with me the image of the God of my childhood, who dwelt in the heavens surrounded by angels playing their harps. According to the song I grew up with, Jesus loved me because I was one of "all the little children of the world." But I had yet to reconcile those words with Gram's God, who poured judgment on the wicked. The old man sitting on the throne with the long, white beard was supposed to have heard my prayers, but I already knew God was no Cosmic Santa Claus. My professors introduced me to a different God: one who liberates the oppressed, speaks for the marginalized, and lifts up the downtrodden. My entire world seemed like a glorious spring day when I finally understood that God would never have punished Mom for anything I did. The theological shift could have been unsettling. Instead, it loosened me from the shackles of a judgmental and vengeful God.

All the while, the preacher's son and I were falling in love. Because I was desperate to be wrapped in the love of another family, our courtship was fast, our engagement faster, and we were married by Thanksgiving. I found temporary relief from my loneliness. My father-in-law nurtured my curiosity about God and encouraged me to consider the vocation of ministry.

The childhood memory of my confirmation and first communion bubbled up and powered my passion for and call to a ministry of sacrament. It was Palm Sunday, 1966, in the large sanctuary of First Methodist Church in Westfield. Mom dressed me in a new blue and white houndstooth suit with a yellow blouse. Kneeling at the same altar rail where I had not received my third-grade Bible, I felt loved and whole, accepted by God as I was without judgment. Confirmation was my touchstone, the moment I first understood whose I was. I belonged to God. Therefore, I could withstand the storm raging around me. From that day forward, the Holy Eucharist held deep meaning for me. As a seminary student, I now understood the sacrament and longed to extend that sense of belonging to others.

*Could I be a conduit for the affirmation of God's promise?*

I wondered what Gram would think. I doubted she would approve. Self-doubt crept in, and I questioned my call.

*Am I worthy? Do I want the life of a pastor, giving my weekends to God?*

At this point, few women were in ministry, and I was not at all sure I was prepared to handle the pushback from people in the pews. Even that concern did not deter me from pursuing what I believed to be a genuine call to ministry. No voice boomed from the heavens. No edict or command from the Divine was handed down to me. Rather, it was a quiet, inner confidence assuring me that this was what I was supposed to do.

Moreover, I was certain that my ministry was to be in higher education, to be a bearer of God's peace and forgiving love in the academic setting, especially to college students. My own vacuum of faith in college reminded me how critical it is for students to have a person of faith, a mentor, someone available and willing to walk with them through a most disruptive and transitional time of life. I finally knew where I was headed and had a map to take me there.

During my second year in seminary, I began to see that my past had equipped me to face the misogyny and hostility towards women I would experience in ministry. One day after class, a classmate propositioned me. Another pressured me not to get married. The pastor who supervised my internship untied the bows on my blouses until I started wearing pullover sweaters. When a visitation team came to the seminary to meet with prospective ordinands, the team leader stood to greet me. He shook my hand, turned to his colleagues, and said, "Wouldn't she be nice to look at even if she didn't have anything to say?"

*Seriously?*

I snapped back at the chortles and nodded at the table. "I wouldn't be going through all of this if I didn't have anything to say."

An older pastor, well-established and well-regarded by his peers, patted me on the head. Another called me a "piece of fluff." They and their colleagues treated the women entering the ministry like naïve little girls. The truth was we were a threat to their status quo, a disruption to their way of doing business. They behaved as though we were invading their club, but the abuse was familiar territory to me, so I held fast to the confidence of my call.

These encounters in seminary were enough to raise red flags, but I ignored them. I endured their gauntlet, got married, had a baby, and graduated. Eight weeks after receiving my diploma, I accepted my appointment to pastor two small churches in northwest Virginia. Still, I was taken aback by the headwinds I faced in the parish. The laity, both men and women, expressed their unease with women in the pulpit. It was not personal—all my clergy sisters shared stories of parishioners behaving as though they were green aliens fresh off the spaceship, planning to take over their small corner of the world.

The day after we moved into the parsonage, Billie appeared at the backdoor, cake in hand.

"Is your mother home?" she inquired.

"Um, no."

"Is she…Are you…" her face flushed as she realized her faux pas.

I giggled, trying to assuage her embarrassment. I took the cake and invited her in for a glass of iced tea. The following Sunday, when the choir director resigned before worship, Billie, a trained church musician, stepped in to fill the void. We became fast friends, which lasted for years until she passed away.

On Monday morning, after my first sermon, I sat down at my desk, ready to make pastoral visits.

*Where does a preacher start to make house calls?*

I had no idea. So, I opened the church directory and started with the As. Mrs. Anderson opened her front door and greeted me with a big smile. She was a kind, salt-of-the-earth woman who poured out her troubles as generously as the sweet tea she decanted into my glass. Her appreciation overflowed. The following Sunday, she and her husband sat in their pew at the back of the church, much to everyone's surprise. After worship, I learned that Mr. Anderson had stood up after worship the Sunday before I arrived and announced to the congregation that he and his wife would not return until "the lady preacher leaves." But there they were. Some called it a coincidence. I called it a gift of the Spirit and saw it as confirmation that God had, indeed, called me to this work.

Several church members appeared at the front door a week later, each carrying a pound of something. One carried butter, another brought flour, and a third carried a bag of sugar. Others brought jars filled with fruits and garden vegetables they had grown and canned themselves. And homemade apple butter, apple sauce, and apple cake—it was apple country.

"We're here to pound you," one of them announced. His voice conveyed his assumption that I understood his meaning and would let them all in the door.

I had never heard of this and was not at all sure I wanted these people in my—their—house. My boundaries were at odds with my attempt to gain pastoral credibility, so I welcomed them in and did my best to extend gracious hospitality, but not without reservation.

*I hope they don't expect me to make them a cake.*

Ministry was not all bad, but sometimes, confirmation of my call was insufficient, and I questioned my resolve. Moving into a parsonage was traumatic for me. I did not want to be told where to live. I did not care for the furniture or how the house was decorated. The house and furnishings were fine; they simply did not suit my taste. I wrestled with it like Jacob with the unknown visitor. When I grumbled to a friend about it, she suggested that my resistance was because, without my parents, I lacked a home. I considered the possibility she could be right. My husband and mother-in-law had told me nightmare stories about some of the parsonages they had lived in. They were alarming emergency flares, but I was a horse with blinders on, and my naivete helped me to ignore them until I stood face to face with the invasion of privacy and unrealistic expectations held by some parishioners.

The honeymoon ended in less than a month. A lay leader in one church threatened me, "If you don't work with me, I will report you to your superintendent." I outmaneuvered him by going to the superintendent first.

I came home one day after making hospital visits to find a couple of kitchen cabinet doors wide open.

*Someone must have a key to the parsonage, and they came in and rummaged around.*

A week or so passed before I locked myself out of the parsonage, not once but twice. I climbed into the house through a window in my office each time. The second time, I knew what was happening.

*I don't want to be here.*

But here I was, at least for now.

# CHAPTER 24

Before I arrived at my first appointment, that is, between April and the end of June, I gave birth to our first child, finished my exams—one from my hospital bed—and moved into a parsonage.

By the time October rolled around, I was depleted from head to toe. All the transitions and adjustments had exhausted me. I was an empty vessel with nothing to offer. When an invitation to area clergy arrived to attend a retreat, I signed on without hesitation.

Thirty of us gathered for a time of spiritual renewal. Together, we shared stories from the "front line," the challenges and blessings of ministry. I was encouraged to discover that my experiences echoed those of my colleagues. I was not alone. We laughed. We cried.

*Rinse. Repeat.*

Our retreat leader read us the story of the woman at the well found in the fourth chapter of John's gospel. He directed us to a time of silent contemplation through guided imagery and urged us to remain in the words and images, to rest in God's safe and secure presence. A well-defined picture of the woman was projected onto the screen of my imagination. She was unwanted. Marginalized. Cast out. Invisible. Her story was personal to me. I resonated with the pain she must have known. Then, I imagined myself standing at the edge of a deep well, peering into the darkness.

*What's down there?*

I looked in and then away, but curiosity pulled at me the same way crabs did when they at the chicken necks in the Creek.

*Do I dare go down there to find out?*

I looked in again and then behind me to see if anyone was watching. The void below was a vast darkness, an enigma, a puzzle waiting to be solved. A flimsy-looking ladder leaned against the lip of the shaft—an invitation into the well.

*This might be a mistake, but I have to go down there.*

With apprehension, I placed my left foot on the first rung, then my right. My eyes focused not below but in front of me as I descended. Ten, twenty, thirty steps? I lost count. The wood was rough on my hands, my knuckles turning white as though I was clinging to my life.

*Am I afraid of falling? What if the ladder breaks?*

I stepped from the last rung and found myself standing in a large, round room with mud walls. A small bonfire was burning in the center of the floor, and an older woman sat beside it; her legs crossed in front of her. She was dressed in a brown tunic with a brown turban wrapped around her head. She looked like a hermit. Her face revealed decades of exposure to the sun. Her wrinkles accounted for years of wisdom. She appeared both weathered and wise. She reminded me of mi abuela.

She dipped her chin, nodding to me a wordless welcome. I sat down across the fire from her and eyed her with suspicion. We exchanged no words but watched the fire together as the flames lapped at the logs. We held a silent vigil until I noticed an unspoken, energetic invitation to be her spiritual companion.

*You can't be my spiritual guide. You're not real!*

I resisted. This was absurd. Ridiculous! I did not learn this in seminary, which made me disinclined to trust it, but her pull was intense. When I let go of my need to understand and accepted her invitation, I understood my work there was done. I rose, returned to the ladder, and climbed back into the "real world."

Though I left the woman in the well, she did not leave me. She accompanied me on my spiritual journey for several years. With each meditation, I found my place in the cavern by the fire, and she was there. She emanated a comforting, reassuring presence and a spiritual energy that supported me in ministry. When I prayed, she was there. As I prepared to preach, she was there. In the silence, her spirit was a source of strength. She was trustworthy, and I was confident she would neither betray nor abandon me.

Six years later, I was pastoring a large congregation in Northern Virginia when I was invited to travel to the Holy Land with a group of colleagues. We began our pilgrimage at the Western Wall, the towering limestone edifice sacred to Jewish men and women around the world for thousands of years. The plaza in front of the Wall is divided by a screen. Women pray on the right side, men on the left; both are furnished with wooden benches and chairs.

I approached the Wall with a group of clergy sisters. Our chatter subsided as we neared the Wall until, at last, we fell into an awe-filled silence. Greenish brown grasses cascaded from the Wall in clumps. Tiny rolls of paper—all inscribed with prayers—were stuffed into the crevices between the rocks and even into the weathered pits in the rocks themselves.

*Where do all these little scraps of paper go? What does one pray for here?*

The question in my head received a blaring, imagined response, "Pray for the peace of Jerusalem."

I backed away from the wall to sit on a bench and closed my eyes to pray for the peace of Jerusalem. Then, I descended the familiar ladder into what I had decided was a kind of cistern. When I landed on the floor, I noticed the fire had dwindled to ashes, and my guide was nowhere in sight. I called to her. There was no response. I twisted my body full circle in search of her. She was not there. My peace evaporated. I bent down to blow on the ashes, hoping for a tiny ember to reignite and restore the flame so she would return. But there were no embers—the fire was extinguished. I called her again. And again. Angst was turning to grief when, in the stillness, I heard her speak the first and only words she would ever say to me.

"You don't need me anymore. You are forgiven."

*What?*

I gasped. Of course, I was forgiven! I knew that. Or did I?

*God did not punish Mom, but am I living a forgiven life?*

I responded silently,

*I DO need you!*

But she was gone. And she was not coming back. Abandoned once again. Before I had time to absorb all of what I was experiencing, the tour guide beckoned us to return to the bus. I opened my eyes and stood, with resignation, then turned my back on the Wall and the generations of prayers, and I boarded the bus. Confusion and dismay overwhelmed me. The familiar numbness of grief descended on me like a pall as we drove through the city on our way to the Garden Tomb.

*What will I do without her?*

The Garden Tomb, pristine, pastoral, and meticulous, is one of the two sites historians claim to be the resting place of the crucified Jesus. We listened as the guide read us the story of Jesus' crucifixion and resurrection. We viewed the empty tomb and shared the Holy Eucharist. Then, as we made our way toward the exit, the guide pointed out a cistern to our left covered by a substantial wooden disc.

*Huh. A cistern. That's odd.*

We were funneled into the gift shop, where I perused books and souvenirs. As I approached the door to leave, I noticed a rack of postcards near the checkout counter. One card grabbed my attention—a picture of the inside of the cistern we had passed—a large, round room with mud-colored walls and a tall wooden ladder. There was no fire in the photo. No older woman sitting on the cistern floor. But there was also no doubt—this was where my spiritual guide had waited for me, comforted and guided me. This was where I prayed for six years.

# CHAPTER 25

My faith was enriched daily in unexpected ways as I allowed the woman in the well to continue with me on my spiritual journey. The experience in the Holy Land settled on me like an intricately woven lace coverlet. It extended my theological understanding and enriched my faith. It opened me to peace in contemplative prayer. People in the pew might have called it my "born again" moment. But the truth was, they could not appreciate my story and, instead, met it with skepticism, even judgment.

"You should never 'empty yourself' because the devil will fill you up," Fred cautioned me.

"The Bible is clear in its condemnation of that!" Bill pressed.

"That's witchcraft," Barbara said.

Their condemnations reflected more disbelief than faith. But I had received spiritual assurance in the cistern, so I held fast to what I knew to be true. As much as I wanted to share the story with Gram, I did not dare. I knew she would dismiss it. She never displayed an ability to accept this kind of transformational moment on my spiritual journey.

My spiritual, mental, and emotional states were all shifting. Perhaps predictably, those changes became bumps in the road. My nine-year marriage was imploding. It had always been on shaky ground. Each of us had brought too much baggage to the relationship and piled onto it the weight of parish ministry and two children. We were in therapy, but the cracks between us were turning into canyons. I am not sure if it was that, or the age of my children, or the weekly therapy sessions, but my carefully constructed cave, which had been slowly eroding since Dad's suicide, was under full assault now. It was being bombarded on all sides. The final phase of deconstruction may have started the day my therapist confronted me.

"Why are you resisting me?"

I had no answer for her. I had no idea what she was talking about.

She pushed me. "You don't know how to ask for what you need."

*I gave up asking for what I need so long ago I don't even know how to identify what my needs are.*

"Your sky is always gray. There is always a cloud over you."

I stared at her, expressionless. She was right, but I did not know what caused it or how to disperse it.

Questions started to bubble up from my subconscious. They forced me to self-examination; they challenged me to dismantle my fortress. My self-assumptions were blowing up. I was desperate to fix "it," whatever "it" was. I believed I was good at "fixing" whatever was broken. The more I looked within, the faster the questions came, and the quicker my walls crumbled. My safe space was collapsing bit by bit, threatening to expose my fragility, vulnerability, and brittle identity to the world. And amidst my own disassembling was my determination to spare our children the cold war I had grown up in.

One morning, my reflection in the mirror raised the first question that set in motion the final collapse of my defenses.

*Why are you always in conflict? Where is your anger coming from?*

Citadel ramparts crashed down around me.

*Why are you so sensitive? Why do you take everything so personally?*

Walls crumbled in front of me.

*Why do you rehearse every wound? Why can't you let things go?*

My protective shelter could no longer stand up to the forces that willed me to find healing. I could see my pain was oozing, bleeding into the world. Even as I struggled to stop it, even when I could see it was damaging my relationships, it grew worse. My nerves were frayed. I was short with my children—scolding them instead of taking the time to sit and listen to them. My parishioners distanced themselves, one telling me I was too angry all the time.

"I am going to call your doctor to get you a prescription for anti-depressants," my therapist said.

Tears poured out. My guts spewed out on the floor. Failure.

"Thank you," I choked on my self-incrimination. But her refusal to give up on me gave me hope.

*Maybe I can be fixed, redeemed.*

The medication reset my brain. At first, I felt disoriented, as though my sense of self was under threat of erasure. I switched to low gear and could not write a sermon or summon the will to preach the following Sunday.

Much to my surprise, I did not care. It made no difference to me that I was, in my mind, failing to do what was expected of me. Two days later, I did not feel quite as low. The dark cloud overhead began to break up. Most remarkable was the realization I had been depressed my entire life and did not know it. Once my body adjusted to the drug, I felt lighter. I laid down the sack of rocks I had carried for over thirty years and struggled to move forward. I tried to keep the four of us together, but even my best efforts could not conceal the truth: the marriage would not be saved.

I was getting better, but I was nowhere close to leaving the forest. After our separation became public, the bishop decided it would be best for me to be assigned to a different church. He was oblivious to my instability and limitations. Waves of insecurity overwhelmed me. No raft was sturdy enough to provide me with the mental, emotional, and spiritual resources I needed to care for a new congregation. My priority was my children, and self-care was critical. I had to know—and honor—my limits. When I learned the receiving community had not been informed that their incoming pastor would be a divorced clergywoman with two young children, any visions I had entertained for an effective ministry sank to the bottom of the creek. I was stuck in the mud without a way out. At my ordination, I promised to go where I was sent. Now the good girl in me tugged at my commitment.

*What am I going to do? I cannot go. What will happen if I refuse?*

Less than two weeks before the moving van arrived, I preached a fiery sermon on Pentecost Sunday and went home to start taking pictures off the walls. That evening, having tucked my children into their beds, I fell into my bed and cried myself to sleep. In the middle of the night, I sat bolt upright, awakened by a haunting voice that said,

"Who do you think you are? You can't do this—not now. You need to take care of yourself and your children."

I did not know where the voice came from but knew I had to obey this phantom, this night visitor. I had to risk this leap of faith without fear of repercussions. It seemed clear that my life depended on it. The following day, I called my superintendent and requested a year of family leave. I hung up my clerical vestments and rebuffed my guilt and shame, the inner voice that told me I was misbehaving, that I was an inconvenience to the system.

*You can't worry about them now. They'll figure it out.*

Rejecting others' expectations, I felt immediate relief—and maybe a bit rebellious. I could breathe. The good girl was set free. Abstention from alcohol was one of the mandates given to ordained clergy, so I went to the grocery store and bought a bottle of wine. A smile coursed across my face and a giggle welled up inside as I checked out. This was a (defiant) freedom I had never known.

I celebrated my liberation but had no plan for an income stream. When I began to wonder how I would feed the children, I assured myself we would be okay. I convinced myself that God would keep us afloat as I swam with the children through uncharted waters. Substitute teaching, baking and selling bread, and a consulting gig put food on our table. War waged in the Middle East, and I prayed for peace without and within as I unpacked a lifetime of unresolved issues with my therapist. But I was still in a vault, locked up tight with no key or combination to get out. I gave my therapist little to work with. She raised questions, but the petrified little girl inside of me was still hard at work, pushing back at every attempt to answer them. It was plain to see how my depression impacted my ministry and marriage, but I was far from understanding how it framed my entire life.

# CHAPTER 26

## Barnacles and Jellyfish

In a world filled with dangers and threats, creatures—even the human variety, especially those traumatized in childhood—develop natural ways to defend and protect themselves.

The dock was supported by dark wood pilings driven into the mud and coated with tar. Over time, hundreds of barnacles made the pilings their homes. Colonies of crustaceans self-cemented for life to the stanchions. Each pole was adorned with creamy white aprons from the mud up to the low tide line, their fragile, feathery wisps protruding and waving with the tide to filter nutrients from the water. To the touch, they were crusty and crunchy. The calcific plates comprising their shells were both defining and protective. An accidental brush against them would cause a bleed. At the same time, they were exposed and vulnerable. A gentle bump from the boat could yield a devastating, fatal blow, crushing the aprons to death. They were at once dangerous and fragile. Razor-sharp and helpless. Treacherous and brittle.

The water transformed into an inviting swimming hole when the summer sun's warmth raised the Creek's temperature. Until the jellyfish arrived with the incoming tide. Where the barnacles were staid and immovable, the jellyfish were fascinating regiments of grace, floating, pulsing, dancing through the water, their tentacle tails drifting behind. They appeared to be phantasms, gentle ghosts of lacy, flimsy filaments. The tendrils were sentinels in search of food and buoys of self-defense, a threat to many a swimmer. A brush with one left a stinging, searing sensation. They were quick to inflict pain upon the unsuspecting, innocent bather. Similar to the barnacles, they were seen as a risk and to be avoided at all costs. They, too, were dangerous and fragile, perfidious and prickly.

# CHAPTER 27

Gram stayed alone on the farm for ten years after Gramps died. She described her loneliness as devastating. A single fish in a tank—her aquarium a shrine of pictures and memories.

Sixty years spanned our ages. Two world wars, a pandemic, and the Great Depression had shaped her worldview. The invention of the gas turbine redefined her generation, and horse-drawn buggies were replaced by automobiles and airplanes. The vacuum cleaner and the electric washing machine reimagined her homemaking. In comparison, my thirty-year lifespan was rather unremarkable. Even with several high-profile political assassinations, a presidential resignation, a failed war, and a successful walk on the moon, my world had not changed as much as hers had.

Too much separated us now. Her constant companions were TV evangelists who shored up her worldview. Meanwhile, my spiritual journey and growing self-awareness were enlarging my heart. All I wanted from her was what I thought I once had—her unconditional love. Approval of my life choices or an expression of pride about my ministry would have been a bonus. But all of that seemed out of reach now. The best she could muster was prayers. My busy life, with a demanding career and children to raise, needed to be prayed for, but I was not sure I wanted her to pray for me.

Gram was in her nineties, and her health was starting to decline. She experienced a couple of episodes of dehydration followed by hospital visits. They led her to agree with Dick she could no longer live on her own. She moved to a nursing home in a town twenty minutes from the farm. Dick and I visited as our time allowed. He still lived and worked in California, and my life was over-scheduled. Our trips to the Shore were infrequent. With each visit, we noticed her gradual physical and mental decline. Conversations were more difficult as her memory faded. She called me Lolly and mistook Dick for Gramps, but she was comforted by words of scripture or a cassette tape of her favorite hymns. She had downloaded the words to those hymns in the database of her mind, accessing them with ease when the music began. She warbled *Come, Thou Fount of Every Blessing*, *Rock of Ages*, and her favorite *Blessed Assurance* without missing a word or a beat, even though her once beautiful soprano voice had turned weak and raspy. She was losing her vigor. We were losing our matriarch.

Dick and I struggled to keep up with the farm. It, too, showed signs of age and deterioration. The paint was fading from the aluminum siding. The grass was overgrown. Barn roofs were sagging. Dock planks were rotting. But we were not ready to let it go. We loved it as much as Gram and Gramps had. Dick spoke of his coming retirement and his hope of spending more time there, but Helen had developed health issues that short-circuited his dream. He wanted me to be the caretaker, but I lacked the time and energy, not to mention the skills, to pick up the slack. That did not stop him from trying to teach me the basics of maintenance.

We stood before the old black oil-burning furnace in the pump house. "Here is the pilot light; this is how you ensure it works as it should."

"This is maintenance and upkeep. I told you I cannot do it. I cannot be responsible for keeping the farm running. We need to find someone else to take care of the place," I begged. We argued. Despite his frustration, I held fast to my limitations.

I was on family leave when Gram drew her last breath. My prayer was that now she was free of the grief that had shut her off from the world, and that she found in her next life both her Herman and her Lolly and, by extension, her peace. A small group of family and friends gathered in the nursing home's community room to remember her. Dick told me I should "say a few words." I found myself walking a tightrope. Given the dissonance that had defined my relationship with her in her last years, I feared I would do her a disservice. But I dug deep into my memories and managed to honor her. We sang *Blessed Assurance* together, and after greeting friends, we drove into town for lunch. I sensed her presence as we sat around the table, recalling the many meals we shared at the farm over the years.

"She washed her money!" a cousin offered.

"And plastic bags," I said, remembering the bags clipped to the back porch railing and left to air dry.

"She took a clean, pressed hanky to a restaurant. At the end of the meal, she pulled it from her oversized blue pocketbook, spread it on the table, and placed all the leftover dinner rolls on it. She wrapped them up and slipped them in her bag, took them home, and served them for breakfast the next morning." Dick shook his head as he laughed.

"She hated fish! If we went to a fish house for dinner, she ordered steak and complained about how poorly cooked it was," I said.

"Don't lick your fingers! She scolded us at every meal," her niece recalled.

"She would slip a five-dollar bill into the apron of the deaf busser at our favorite restaurant. She had a beautiful smile and a wonderful laugh, but she sure was stubborn," I said.

There were nods around the table. More memories gave way to laughter. Before long, with clean plates and full stomachs, we had grieved well. Gram's ashes were sealed tight in a light blue urn and placed on top of the bookcase in the den at the farm to be interred at a later time.

Dick made occasional trips to the Shore after Gram died. I joined him whenever my schedule allowed, and we did our best to complete basic chores and maintenance. We did what we could to keep the farm from falling into complete disrepair, but we were fighting a losing battle from a distance. Dick found a young man to live in the farmhouse in exchange for keeping the grass mowed in the summer and the heat on in the winter. He was a bachelor and a Shore native who did what was asked of him, but the farm needed more. And when Dick's health began to fail, it was time for the difficult conversation about this last, ailing kin—the farm.

"How much work and money can we afford to put into keeping up this place?"

"It is turning into a money pit, and no one is there to enjoy it."

A faint current of grief flowed between our words like the tide in the Creek.

*What will life be without the farm? It has been our touchstone. Our safe space. Our heaven.*

The heartache hanging over our conversation was the darkest of clouds. We were losing another family member. Another body part was being severed. Wincing as the words left my mouth, I told him, "It is time to let someone else love it."

As hard as it was to acknowledge, as much as he hated to, he surrendered and conceded it was time to let it go.

# CHAPTER 28

It took Dick eight years to put the farm up for sale. By 2000, I had remarried and moved with my son to live with my husband in North Carolina. My daughter was in college.

Did I volunteer to clean out the farmhouse, or did it become apparent no one would if I did not? Did I consult with Dick, or did I resign myself to do it because it needed to be done? However it developed, I saw it as both a labor of love and part of the process of letting it go. I called my friend, Sherry, who knew her way around antiques, and I enlisted the help of my daughter. Together, we descended on the farm for a week in the spring armed with gloves, pails, brushes for cleaning, and boxes and newspapers for packing.

I was unprepared for what we saw when we rounded the bend in the drive. The farm had fallen from bad to worse inside and out. Weeds choked the rose bushes to death. The birdbath was toppled over, its bowl shattered. The white aluminum siding was bleached to a silvery-gray. Mice were kings and queens of the barns, and the black snakes owned the trees. Indoors, the paint had taken leave of the ceiling in chunks to reside on the radiators. Layers of dust covered the furniture like lace doilies. Mice had claimed the house as their second realm, building nests in desk drawers and coat pockets.

We donned gloves and protective masks and got to work. At the end of the week, what was left of a life?

We sent old books, decades of *National Geographic* and *News and World Report* magazines, dated papers, and worn towels to the dump. We set aside cookware, usable furniture, and linens in good condition to donate to Goodwill.

Sherry took Gram and Gramps' bedroom suite home to give to her son. I was comforted knowing it would be given new life and loved in its new environs. She took Gramps' desk, assorted trinkets, bone china, and glassware for her consignment shop. I thought it reasonable to get a little money for the nicer items.

Dick wanted the hunting rifle Gramps' had used to scare away stray dogs. And the World War One Luger Pistol I found buried under pillows and bedspreads in a drawer in their dressing room. My cousin wanted one of the Tiffany glass lampshades. Helen was supposed to get the forty-pound marble bust of Joan of Arc, but no one wanted to bear the shipping cost.

We left a few necessities—the sleep sofa, a few pots and pans, a couple of plates, and some flatware—in case we had reason to return.

We were skillful and careful in packing the back of a U-Haul with what was left for me to take home. I had an emotional attachment to the mahogany sideboard and curved glass cabinet Gram had bought for fifty cents at Goodwill. They were anchors in the dining room and embodied cherished memories of the scores of meals we had shared there. The small, glass-paned cabinet where Gramps had stored his slides was precious, and I imagined it as a treasured addition to my study. There were mirrors I was not ready to part with—one hung by the front door, and another hovered over the fireplace. I packed the butterfly plates and bowls that Gram had labeled "very valuable" in case my daughter wanted them. We squeezed pink-flowered woolen blankets and goose-down pillows in all the empty spaces of the van to keep articles from bouncing and breaking.

I slid one last box, filled with photos, postcards, and a few documents—birth certificates, marriage certificates, and a hand-typed family lineage—onto the cab floor. We closed the door, locked the house up tight, and with silent melancholy, I climbed into the truck to head south down the Shore one more time. Memories rushed in with the tide as I drove the truck over the bridges and through the tunnels. Crossing the final bridge, I imagined Mom standing at the rail, scattering her ashes into the wind.

As difficult as it is to bury a body, it is harder still to separate ourselves from what is left of a life. We cling to the material, holding on to the spirits they represent. So, I surrounded myself with objects guaranteed to conjure the best memories. I placed them around our home with care, holding them close, and with each glance at them, I willed the ghosts to come back to life. These familiar "friends" embraced me and, in a way, welcomed me home.

Five months later, I heard the roar of semi-tractor trailer trucks echoing through the pines of the Shore. There were three, maybe four of them. The engines groaned when the gears shifted. As they approached, the din of tires on the road swelled to a racket. I had heard this clamor before, but the volume was ratcheted up this time—a lot. The trucks were closer. And there were more of them.

*Are they headed to the farm?*

Unless they drove past the drive or turned back, they would soon careen down the sandy lane, past Gramps' speed limit sign and the trumpet vines, past the persimmon and cherry trees, and up to the farmhouse at the edge of the Creek.

A magnificent magenta and purple sky was giving way to a starry night. The great blue heron strutting along the edge of the cove took flight and skimmed the top of the black water before taking flight to find its way to its night perch in a pine tree. I was preparing for bed in what I still thought of as Gram and Gramps' dressing room. From these windows, I knew I could see the intruders if, and when, they reached the clearing a football field's distance away. I longed for them to pass by the drive and head down to Burton's farm or beyond. But I knew if the trucks came around the bend and through the clearing, they were here for a reason.

The cacophony shattered the peace and serenity of the farm. The noise was exaggerated beyond my ability to withstand it. My apprehension increased in proportion to the volume of the noise. The louder the noise, the closer they were. The closer they were, the more danger they represented.

*Who are they? What do they want?*

I wracked my brain, trying to imagine answers to those questions. They had to know there were no valuables here. The house had been empty for months. All that remained were the bare essentials. No riches. No gems. Still, I could not shake the notion they were there to collect a precious treasure. And I had no way to defend myself. Gramps' guns were gone—not that I knew how to use them. Gram had sold the boat. There was no escape by water. I was defenseless and trapped like a muskrat in one of Gramps' cages.

I could see the headlights flickering now as the trucks made their way towards the house. They were going to outnumber me. They could overcome me and claim what they came for without resistance. I was paralyzed—growing more and more frightened as the four unmarked, gray tractor-trailers labored through the clearing.

When the drivers jumped from the cabs, it was too dark to make out their faces. The security light illuminated the scene enough for me to see them at all. They left the engines running. They yelled at one another as they brandished their weapons. There was much I could not see or understand, but I knew I was in grave danger.

*They mean business. They are armed and dangerous.*

They were positioned and ready to storm the house.

My breathing was shallow and fast. My pulse pounded hard in my head. I had only one recourse, so that's what I did: I woke myself up.

*I have had versions of this dream before. Several times.*

None had been this threatening. At first, the noise of a single truck pierced the silent night. It never neared the farm. But this dream brought more trucks with heightened intensity. They were getting closer. This was different. Louder. In my space. With faces and weapons. And a message.

"You have left something undone."

What? What did I fail to take care of when we packed and closed up the house?

The following day, I phoned Sherry, and we agreed to meet at the farm two weeks later. We arrived to find the Creek as still as glass. Even the air itself seemed unwilling to move. Geese paraded along the bank across the cove. An osprey perched on her nest atop the light pole. She should have already left for the winter, but instead, she appeared to be a guard—staying at the farm long enough to ensure my work there was done.

I pulled a shovel and toolbox from my trunk, and we walked around the house to find the plaque over Mom's grave buried under weeds. When the shovel pierced the sandy soil, my heart suddenly softened.

*This is why I am here.*

The treasure I retrieved from the garden had been underground for twenty-five years. I pulled it from the hole, brushed the sandy soil from the Revere Ware pot, and walked along the drive to where the cock-eyed, chipped, and time-worn tombstones still stood. I removed the package from the pot, tore away the tape, the plastic, and the paper. I shook the box, and the contents rattled.

Sherry's face twisted. "I didn't think ashes made noise."

I pulled a hammer and screwdriver from my toolbox and used them to pry and pound, wiggle and fidget. After twenty minutes, I lifted the lid to see inside. Gray ashes. White chunks of bone.

*Mom is thirsty.*

Urn in hand, I walked over to the edge of the Creek while Sherry stayed back, watchfully waiting as she leaned against the locust tree once home to the old basketball backboard and scores of cicada shells. Mom and I stepped into the marsh grass onto the small dock she had built three decades before. Beyond the dock's planks, just under the water's surface, lay the old car tires she had dropped into the mud to create an oyster bed. This was her spot. Hers alone. She cultivated oysters there, and now, the black, gray, and white shells clinging to the slippery black rubber were there to receive her.

I stood on the weathered wood, tipped the box slowly, and watched as a gentle breeze carried the ashes and placed them softly on the water. Mom found her final resting place. She was where she had long wanted to be. At last, she slept in the water, in peace upstream from the Bay. I hoped some of her ashes would float downstream to her chosen destination.

As the osprey swooped low over the cove and out to the open water of the Creek, I wept.

I never dreamed of the trucks again.

# CHAPTER 29

## Dreams

Some say dreams carry little meaning. They are mere rehearsals of our awakened lives. After the truck dream and Mom's "proper" burial, I embraced a different perspective and found myself drawn to the historical record.

Hebrew Scripture is infused with nocturnal visions. In the book of Daniel, King Nebuchadnezzar sought out someone to interpret one which troubled him. He sent for magicians, enchanters, and sorcerers to find one who could tell him the dream's meaning. The problem was he could not recall it, so no one was summoned who could satisfy his wish. He commanded all the wise men of Babylon to be killed. One of them, Daniel, begged for time, and the mystery was revealed to him in a night vision.

Standing before the King, he said, "No wise men, enchanters, magicians, or diviners can show the King the mystery that the King is asking, but there is a God in heaven who reveals mysteries…This mystery has not been revealed to me because of any wisdom that I have more than any other living being, but in order that the interpretation may be known to the King and that you may understand the thoughts of your mind." (Daniel 2:27-28a; 30).

From Babylon to Greece to Rome, from Daniel to the Apostle Paul, ancient cultures believed dreams were essential for the divine to communicate with the human imagination. Native Americans have long embraced them as a gift of the Great Spirit, a source of wisdom. They have been appreciated as symbolic language from Sigmund Freud to Carl Jung. Even Abraham Lincoln wondered if God speaks to people in dreams. After having a prescient dream of his own assassination, Lincoln told Ward Hill Lamon, his bodyguard, friend, and biographer,

> "If we believe the Bible, we must accept the fact that, in the old days, God and his angels came to men in their sleep and made themselves known in dreams."[1]

I have come to believe that we too easily dismiss the gift of our dreams. What we do with them is what empowers us to live fully conscious lives.

[1] William J. Wolf, Lincoln's Religion (Philadelphia: Pilgrim Press, 1970), 29.

# CHAPTER 30

Nine years after leaving the farm, I took down from the attic the box of pictures and papers I had brought home with me in the U-Haul after clearing out the farmhouse. Jeffrey and I had been married for almost ten years, and I wanted to introduce him to a piece of my past. I plowed through the box in search of an old photo. The first picture I came across was of Gram, Gramps, Mom, and me on the night of my high school graduation. Another person had been in the photo, but all that was left to identify him were his untucked shirt and baggy pants—his face had been torn out. Gram's hatred for my father was real.

*You can cut him out of a photo, but you cannot erase him from my life.*

Determined not to spend time revisiting that painful part of my past, I burrowed further and uncovered three familiar photos. Black-and-white images of what must have been a stunning flower garden. Zinnias. Dahlias. Sunflowers. Framed by a stacked stone wall across the back and along the far side. My inner child wanted to paint the flowers fuchsia pink, crimson red, ivory white, and buttery yellow. Any color but gray. Gram's handwriting on the back of one picture located the garden in Visby, Sweden, on the island of Gotland. "This is the garden of Aunt Annie Quiander. She stayed on here after her parents died."

A second photo of the same garden was taken from a different angle and showed the back of a two-story house with a tile roof and two chimneys. A bank of windows overlooked the garden. The inscription on the back of the photo read, "Dear Janice, this is the rear view of your Great-Great Grandmother's home."

The third photo also displayed the garden, and to the left of it was a white-washed carriage house with a wide entry door and two small windows. A massive rock outcropping swelled up in the background, overshadowing the house. There was no inscription on the back.

Along with the photos, there was a sepia-toned postcard of a streetscape with a church steeple hovering in the distance. Words in the lower right corner located the picture: "VISBY Norro Kyrkogaten" (North Church Street).

It was addressed to my grandmother, with a message that began, "Dear Emily." The remainder of the Swedish text was indecipherable, except for the closing salutation: "Love, Hulda."

I rummaged deeper into the box until I found a folded piece of paper, titled,

EMILY JACOBSEN QUINN - FROM MEMORY, April 1975

The words on the page instantly conjured up memories of those hot, humid nights on the farm when the windows were open, and the lights were out to dissuade the midges from sneaking through the screen. Nights when Gram droned on about her history, and I yawned and rolled my eyes before nodding off. Just then, I wanted those evenings back. I wanted to hear the elders tell all of their stories.

Gramps' niece recorded this brief pedigree five months before Mom died. When I understood this history before me, my heart filled with gratitude.

> Maternal grandparents-Lawrence and Annie Mortenson Thompson of Qvia Farm, Gotland, Sweden (religion-Lutheran). They took the last name "Qviander" for the farm on which they lived... After retiring, the couple bought a house in the City of Visby, Gotland...
> Children of Lawrence and Annie Mortenson Thompson:
> Rudolf, who also had one son named Rudolf
> Annie Bernardina, unmarried
> Hulda Fredricka Elise, unmarried
> Emily Dora Christine, unmarried
> Elin Garda Augusta, who had a son named David Alma, who has one son named Al Denny. He has sons, Robert and Al.
> Hilda Laura Maria married Henry Jacobsen, a Dane... Her two children were Walter Henry Jacobsen and Emily Maria Jacobsen Quinn. Her two grandchildren are Richard Dunraven Quinn and Laura Choate Quinn Rivero. Her great-grandchildren are Rick Quinn, Patricia Quinn, and Janice Rivero.

The roots of my family tree were deeper than I had ever imagined. And for the first time, I understood the tree was still alive, and I was attached to it. I was captivated by the story in my hands. It was Gram's story, Mom's story, and mine, too. Curiosity grabbed me and would not let me go. I wanted to know more of this place.

I was scheduled to attend an international conference for campus ministry professionals in Finland over the summer. Jeffrey and I decided to seize the opportunity to explore Sweden and investigate my heritage. As we settled into our seats, preparing for takeoff, I whispered to Jeffrey, "I will be happy to find a tombstone."

He smiled in recognition but dared not dash my hopes. I wanted to be realistic with my expectations, so I set the bar low. Without contacts on the ground and no knowledge of the language, it may well have been a fool's errand, but I was foolish enough to hope we would stumble upon something, anything, that would locate my ancestors and connect me to this motherland. A tombstone would be enough.

The photos, postcard, and lineage were tucked into the pocket of my carry-on bag as we landed in Visby, the largest city on the island of Gotland, "God's land." The Maine-shaped island sits in the middle of the Baltic Sea like a pearl emerging from its shell. It is steeped in rich Viking history, strategically positioned in the middle of the Nordic shipping lanes. Visby, nicknamed the "City of Roses," with its red tile rooftops and ancient cathedral spires, is the best-preserved medieval city in Scandinavia. Its ringmur, the Ring Wall, built in the 13th and 14th centuries, is an essential part of the Visby World Heritage Site.

We arrived on a beautiful June afternoon. The sky was deep blue and dotted with scattered clouds. The warm sunshine and a cool breeze from the sea provided a perfect day for our exploration. As soon as we unpacked our bags, I approached the hotel concierge. "Could you please direct us to the city records office?"

The language barrier proved significant, but we managed. Jeffrey and I set out on foot, exploring the ancient city along our way. We paused at cathedral ruins and ducked into ancient churches still in use. We wandered narrow, cobblestone streets lined with shops and row houses. We arrived at our destination after an hour but found no indication of the office we were looking for. A hospitable, young Swede descended the stairs as we tried to determine our next move.

"Do you speak English?"

"Yes. Can I help you?"

"We are looking for the City Records Office."

"Ah. Yes. It has moved to a new building outside the city walls."

"How far away?"

"About a forty-minute walk," he replied.

"Thank you."

Jeffrey and I decided to take a cab.

The car bumped along the narrow streets and through an archway in the wall where a hefty gate once stood to protect the city residents from attack. The driver dropped us off in front of a large, contemporary building. The sign in front pointed us around the side to the door marked "Postkontor" (Records Office). The door was locked, and I could see no lights on inside. Office hours posted next to the door told us what we already knew: they were closed on ÖNSDAG (Wednesday). It was Wednesday. And the cab was gone.

"What do you want to do?" Jeffrey wondered aloud.

"What do I want to do? I want to come back tomorrow!" I snapped back. I was on a mission. This was nothing more than a minor delay. The sign said the office was scheduled to open at nine the following day, and I intended to be there soon after the doors opened.

We meandered down the hill, and as we approached the walled city, we marveled at the awe-inspiring land and seascape. The two-mile-long, thirteen-foot-high medieval stone wall extended down to the sea, its towers rising to meet the sky. The island's coast yielded to the Baltic and stretched westward as far as we could see. The beauty was pristine.

The following day, we debated renting a car, but without driver's licenses, we were forced to set out again on foot. When we departed the walled city, it was morning rush hour. Cars and trucks whizzed past us as we attempted to navigate the narrow footpath that ran parallel to the highway. It was hot. The climb was steep. We hailed the next cab that came along.

This time, when we arrived, the door was unlocked, and the lights were on inside. We entered the records office, and Jeffrey held the door for the blonde-haired, barrel-shaped man who walked behind us. The office was lined with shelves of record books. A slender, balding, older man in a red plaid shirt and threadbare wheat-colored sweater vest stood behind the desk. His knowledge of English went no further than "hello." My attempts to communicate with him seemed futile. I wanted someone to see the cartoon bubbles coming from my mouth and translate my English words into Swedish.

He could not even decipher the message inscribed in Swedish on the back of the postcard. My hope waned and my spirit sagged like a clothesline burdened with wet laundry.

*There will be no tombstone for me.*

We were about to leave when the man who had followed us in swiveled his chair away from the microfiche screen to face us.

"What are you trying to do?"

*His English is perfect!*

I showed him the photos, the postcard, and the descendants as I knew them.

"I think I can help you. Let me finish this first."

He pivoted back to his work. Less than five minutes later, he stood before me.

"How can I help you?"

"I'm looking for information about my ancestors." I handed him the paper with the list of names, and he returned to his chair and made haste through the archives. It was evident he knew his way around them quite well.

A few more minutes passed before he said, "I think I found it."

"Honestly?" My ears perked up, my voice lilted, and my hope rushed back in.

He clicked "print," and in a flash, he handed me photocopies of church records that spewed from the Ricoh printer on five eleven-by-fourteen sheets of clean white paper.

"Using the name Lars, Swedish for Lawrence, and Annie Qviander, I found the membership rolls from Martebo Kyrka, the small parish church in Binge, fourteen or fifteen miles north of here. My name is Mats, by the way."

"Wow! I'm Jan. This is my husband, Jeffrey."

Mats walked me through the pages line by line, pointing out each child's name and birthdate, all corresponding to Gram's memory.

He took the postcard from my hand and examined the message. "It's about shoes. But I can't make it out. I think she had dyslexia. And she is the child whose grades were poor. In those days, the church was also the school. Most of the children did very well. But, look, this one, Hulda. She did not perform well."

He pointed to her grades in the church record—one mystery solved. We could see from the records Lars and Annie had sold the farm, left Binge, and moved into Visby, just as Gram had said. We continued our conversation as we walked out the door.

"Thanks so much for your help." I did not have much, but I already knew more than before—maybe enough to find what I was looking for.

We turned to walk down the hill when Mats called out, "Hey! Do you want to see if we can find it?"

"Sure!" I replied without hesitation.

*Maybe I'll find that tombstone after all.*

I creased myself into the front seat of Mats' well-worn, navy-blue Subaru. Jeffrey crawled into the back behind Mats. My quest was given a second life, and I was optimistic again, eager to see what we might find. With help from this new acquaintance, I started to believe that I might just uncover more of my ancestral mystery.

Five minutes up the road, Mats made a sharp left turn onto a narrow dirt road flanked on both sides by tall grass.

"I want to show you this."

No sooner had we left the pavement than I heard Mom's voice.

*"What part of 'don't get in cars with strangers' have you forgotten?"*

My heart plunged to the soles of my feet.

*What was I thinking? Our children will never know what happened to us.*

I caught a glimpse of Jeffrey's wide-open eyes, his head wagging, as the path opened onto a large, flat field. The view was spectacular. To the left, the walled city. Ahead of us, the pristine blue Baltic Sea.

*Well, it's a beautiful sight to see before we die.*

A twelve or thirteen-foot pillar stood in the middle of the field. I could imagine no reason for it to be there until Mats said, "Do you know what they used to do here?"

Before I unraveled my tongue from the back of my throat, he answered his own question. "This is where they executed the criminals. You can still find bones here. Want to look for some?"

My head was spinning. Panic was mounting. I was more afraid we were destined not to leave this field alive, but hedging my bets, I said, "No, thanks. I'm good."

Jeffrey shook his head in the backseat, affirming my vote. Mats looked a bit thwarted and shrugged his shoulders. But he turned the car around and headed us back towards the highway, while I let out a long-held breath and willed my heart back into my chest.

"Now, we need to find people to talk to." Mats revealed his strategy for finding the farm.

We came upon a doubled-over man hobbling down the road with the help of a cane. Mats thought he might be able to help us, so he pulled the car over and jumped out to speak with him. A moment later, he climbed back behind the wheel. "He recently moved in with his daughter. He doesn't know the area at all."

We came upon a stone church: Martebo Kyrka. Mats drove into the churchyard and turned off the engine.

"I'm going to see if I can find a family name on a tombstone in the cemetery," I said, stretching my legs out of the front seat.

I wound my way between the rows of gray, weathered stones, some standing, others sunken into the ground and covered with weeds. None of them displayed a familiar name.

Curious to see inside the church, I tested the doorknob. I was surprised to find it unlocked, and I accepted the unspoken invitation to walk into the ancient Lutheran sanctuary. The room smelled of sweet incense. A five-foot-long replica of a Viking ship hung from the rafters over the pews on the left. Aged wooden planks led to the nave and the baptismal font on the right. The imposing, cold, gray stone bowl, carved around the edge, stood over three feet tall and two feet across.

*My ancestors worshiped here. They were baptized here.*

I ran my hand around the etched edges of the bowl. A holy shiver ran through me and tears welled up. The Christian sacrament of baptism bound me to this place and to them.

*This was so much more than a tombstone!*

But this was not the holy grail, so we twisted ourselves back into the car and continued down the two-lane road. Mats rounded the corner at the sign pointing to Binge. We were getting close. Hope floated up inside me as I gazed out the car window on the open field that stretched back to a grove of pine trees. The geography felt familiar and evoked recollections of a memorable stomping ground.

"This reminds me of the Eastern Shore," I said to Jeffrey, glancing back at him.

*Gram was never here. How could she have known her piece of heaven was so similar to her motherland?*

We continued on until, out of my left eye, I noticed a woman weeding her front garden.

"Mats, maybe she can help us." I pointed to her.

He pulled to the side of the narrow lane. "Wait here!" He leaped from the Subaru and sprinted across the yard.

The garden was filled with pink, white, and red blossoms, and the yard was littered with children's toys. I watched as he spoke to her, and then, together, they went inside the plain, wood-framed house. Jeffrey and I waited. And waited.

*I have to pee.*

Mats emerged after ten minutes—maybe it was five but felt like twenty—my bladder was the one counting. He puffed his cigarette as he rushed towards the car. He poked his head through the window with a grin, his blonde hair blown back and a glimmer in his eye. He radiated the energy of a young boy on Christmas morning. "This is it!" The thrill in his voice was genuine.

Another chill ran down my spine. I could not believe it.

We pulled ourselves from the car and trailed Mats into the house. He introduced us to Marta, who invited us in. She let me use her bathroom (*first things first, thanks be to God*) and served us tea. She was gracious, kind, and hospitable. Then, with Mats translating, she showed us a hardbound book with a red cover. The pages documented the ownership history of all the farms on the island, going back several generations. She opened it and flipped to the page titled BINGE. Translated from Swedish, the first paragraph read,

> In 1896 Emrick Hallgren purchased ¼ Binge Farm from Lars Qviander. The now-deserted farmland is still called Qviandersgarten.

Astonishment swallowed my words whole.

Marta invited us to walk out to Qviandersgarten. Jeffrey and I surveyed the property for a long time. Rocks outlined where the foundation of the house once stood. A large, smooth stone marked the site of the well—their water source. A dilapidated wooden barn edged an open field. I was home. This was home to my ancestors. I wanted to sprawl flat on the ground and soak up all the history in the soil that supported my weight. We took some pictures and strolled back to the house. Without adequate words, I thanked Marta for receiving our intrusion into her day with such grace. She was honored to have been of help.

We were about to collapse into the car again when Mats looked over the hood with a mischievous smile. "Shall we look for the house in Visby? I think we can find it!"

Now, I was confident we would not be sacrificed in the open field to the gods of the Baltic Sea. We found the ancestral farm. Finding the house in the photos would be icing on the cake. "Let's do it!" I said.

We retraced our path back into Visby. The car shook as it coursed the cobblestone streets of the walled city. Stucco houses framed our path, their facades painted in muted shades of yellow, tan, and gray. The colors preserved an ancient dignity amidst the modern telephone poles, power lines, and streetlights. The air was electric.

The three-story, butter-yellow house stood taller than the others around it. It was so large it looked out of place in this row of otherwise quaint, two-story structures. A single stone step led to an olive-green front door flanked by matching green shuttered windows.

There was a short, gravel drive to the left of the house. Mats pulled in and parked the car. I took the photos from my pocket. Standing in front of us was the same carriage house, its metal roof replaced with red tile and a small coach light installed beside the door. The picture had not changed much; the semblance was remarkable, though almost a century separated the past and present. A white facade, a wide entry with a door of horizontal planks, and windowpanes that appeared to be original from the 1920s. The distinctive, dark gray rock outcrop behind the house still loomed large. But the once magnificent flower garden was now a flat, gravel parking area. The stacked stone wall that once edged the garden remained.

A woman approached us as I took pictures. "May I help you?"

I introduced myself. "This is the house where my great-great grandparents once lived. We have come from the U.S. to see if we could find it." I showed her the pictures of the house and garden.

"My name is Miriam."

I gasped.

*Miriam—the name of Jeffrey's older daughter. Another "fluke!"*

Miriam's smile was warm and genuine. "The house now belongs to a wealthy businessman who lives in Stockholm. He comes here in the summers, but he is away this week. I rent the carriage house from him. Would you like to see inside?"

I pulled back at her kind offer. In my mind, I had already overstepped a boundary, so I made a swift emotional retreat and declined her invitation.

I went back to the front of the house. When I turned toward the city center, I gazed at a streetscape that stunned me, though by this time, it should not have. It was my Wizard of Oz moment: the scene turned from black and white to technicolor. The sepia-toned picture on the postcard was transformed into pale-beige and yellow house fronts along the narrow street that led to the white arch, which led to the churchyard. Svenska Kyrka, St. Mary's Cathedral, stood before me, boasting the same unique black bell tower, red tile roofs, and clerestory windows in the old postcard.

History came to life. All the little pieces I found in the box at home fell together. I was awed, overwhelmed by grace. For a moment, time stood still, and I did not want it to start again. I was connected to the land. Tethered by time. Bound together by the waters of baptism. I was whole.

We took Mats to lunch and marveled at the serendipity of the day. I considered him God-sent. He was pleased to have been the key to my successful quest. We assured him I would have returned home empty-handed without his assistance. We said our goodbyes with deep appreciation, but a twinge of sadness welled up in me as I watched him stroll across the plaza toward his car.

*He gave me more than he knows. And I will never see him again.*

Hours later, Jeffrey and I wandered the gaslit streets near our hotel, in search of a simple supper. The closest restaurant did not suit us; its menu was more elaborate and expensive than we were in the mood for. We strolled farther, enjoying the pleasant evening, until we found an intimate outdoor cafe serving hotdogs and öl (beer). It was the perfect way to end the day. Adrenaline had driven us since dawn. Fatigue was creeping in. We were prepared to turn in early, but as we stepped back onto the ancient street, Jeffrey noticed a man riding away on a bike. "Mats!" he yelled.

The biker stopped and turned to look. A grin cracked his dimples, and he whipped his bike around. My body shuddered. My first thought was that he was stalking us. But my apprehension flew away before it could take hold of me.

"I was looking for you! This is for you," he said. He pulled a large manila envelope from under his arm and handed it to me.

*What could this be?*

I opened it and pulled out three small, pastel watercolor paintings of Visby landmarks.

"My father painted them. I want you to have them."

They were lovely. His generosity touched me. I reached in to extract what else was in the envelope: a set of papers stapled together.

As I opened them, Mats confessed his motive for hunting us down. "When I got home, I did more digging and found this," he said, pointing at the pages in my hands.

The top of the first page, in boldface type, read,

ANTAVLA (Pedigree).

Then followed the name Hilda Laura Maria Larsdotter. Hilda, my great-grandmother. The first branches were Hilda's parents,

Father: Lars Ferdinand Qviander,
born March 16, 1834, Väte, Sweden.
Mother: Anna Maria Mårtensdotter (later Mortenson),
born February 2,
1837, Hangvar, Sweden.

My tree grew and grew. The roots dug deep into the ground of my story and filled not one, not two, but eight pages, until I found myself staring at the name of an ancestor nine generations removed.

Jon Mikaelsson, died 1632.

What do you say when you find your roots and discover how deep they run? I held centuries of tombstones in my hands and was awestruck. A vibrant, spiritual energy coursed through my veins. I could not locate the words I needed to say, but Jeffrey found his.

"God is really into you!"

"Huh," I replied. I was left speechless by the way the day had unfolded. His explanation seemed as good as any.

We set out for Finland the next day. We soared over Visby, its red tile roofs, church spires, and ringmur fading below us. That was when I found my words. "I was looking for my ancestors, but my ancestors were looking for me."

✧

It is said that everyone has three deaths. The first is when the body yields itself to the universe. The second is when the body is lowered or scattered to its final resting place. The third is when your name is spoken for the last time. Jon Mikaelsson and his descendants were resurrected and spared their final death.

# CHAPTER 31

Two years later, having claimed my familial inheritance, a restlessness overcame me. After twenty years in higher education ministry, I sensed God calling me down a different path. I did not know where or to what, but I knew it was time to move on. Without a plan, I took another leap of faith and stepped away from a career I had loved. I pushed the pause button on my life only to realize how laser-focused I had been for over fifty years. I now understood what Dick had meant when he told me I was "driven like (your) father." My years had been filled with church and children, driven by ambition and the need to be seen, heard, and taken seriously. There had been little room for music or dancing, laughter or joy, relaxation or revelry. Life was heavy and very serious—more burden than delight.

It was time for me to pull up the anchor and look for what Gramps would have called a "new fishing hole." I did not know how to do it. Ministry had defined me. It had stabilized me and kept me grounded. It moored me to my internal shoreline. My resignation loosened me from the church to seek a new arena for ministry. It was a shock to discover a pastor's skill set does not translate well in the marketplace. After fourteen rejections and feeling like a boat in drydock, I put my job search on hold.

The words of the Psalmist echoed in my head. "Be still and know that I am God" (Psalm 46:10a).

*Easy for you to say.*

It was a test to let go of my inner drive to do, a spiritual discipline to allow myself just to be. The children were gone—our nest was empty. Jeffrey was still teaching. I was at least five years from drawing Social Security. And I was not ready to retire—I had more to contribute to the world.

*What on God's green earth am I going to do?*

I spent too much time browsing the internet with a dull mind. I was a boat adrift at sea. Then, one afternoon, while browsing real estate websites, I came across a house that looked oddly familiar. The outline and window placement nudged a memory from my childhood. To the left of the house stood a magnificent magnolia, and beyond it, there was water. I shook my head and rubbed my eyes.

*This cannot be what I think it is.*

The closer I examined the image, the more different the house seemed from my memory. This house had eggshell white siding, not snow white, not even the weathered gray that I recalled. A pristine landscape transformed once weed-filled garden beds. A crushed shell driveway stretched across the front of the house. Everything was well manicured. And the picture reeled me in like a fish on a hook. I clicked on the photo to see others.

Inside, a beautiful, black, baby grand piano sat in the living room in place of a brown tapestry-covered chair. A painting hung over the fireplace instead of a mirror. A large, shiny, stainless-steel side-by-side refrigerator freezer stood in place of an old yellow refrigerator in the kitchen. Warm, dark wood was swapped for the floor's cracked and warped blue linoleum. The floor plan had been changed enough to confuse me.

*Am I trying to make myself believe this is the farmhouse?*

When I looked past the furniture, I saw it. Enormous windows circumscribed every room and provided clear views of the water beyond. The beauty of the Creek inviting itself indoors filled my eyes with tears.

*It IS the farmhouse! It is beautiful!*

I continued scrolling through the photos to see more changes. The peeling pink paint in Gram and Gramps' room had been painted over with a cool shade of green. Gram's sewing machine in the corner was replaced with a crib. The dressing room and bathroom were redone to include a stacked washer/dryer. A door from the bedroom opened to a renovated balcony that spanned the length of the house. I walked virtually onto the balcony and noticed an inground pool, a pool house, and a rebuilt dock with a boatlift and a stainless-steel counter for cleaning fish.

*This is incredible.*

I could not believe my eyes. But after the serendipity of Visby, I knew this was trustworthy. Shock waves coursed through my spirit. New life energized me like a garden after the rain.

*Someone DID love it. They restored it to life. Resurrection.*

In my delight, I heard the siren call me home. The farm was for sale, but the price was prohibitive, and we would never move there anyway. Nevertheless, my longing to return to the Shore welled up in me like a tidal wave pushing me to dry land.

*I have to see it. I have to go back.*

My calendar was clear of commitments, so I arranged to visit a friend who was spending her summer on the Shore. Two days later, I was packed and ready to go. I kissed Jeffrey goodbye. "I wish you could go with me," I said, wanting a companion on the journey. He was not teaching over the summer. He could afford the time.

"I think this is something you need to do yourself."

*Huh. That's an interesting response. What does he know that I don't? Or is he simply not interested?*

His words and the mystery they held weighed on me as I struck out on the five-hour drive to the Shore. I crossed the state line into Virginia and, miles down the road, passed by the exit I had taken so many times on my way to college. I drove through the Hampton Roads tunnel before turning north, my anticipation growing with each mile. Heaven on earth was whispering to me, and as the tires rolled off the last bridge and onto the Shore, I found myself on holy ground once again. It had been too long—ten years. I filled my torso with salt air. Another forty minutes and I would be home. I passed the white church where Gram and Gramps worshiped for twenty years. And the small yellow house on the hill where Miss Hattie once lived. Left at the Post Office. One more left onto the narrow county road where the loblolly pines first overwhelmed me. In an instant, there was an unexpected internal shift.

*I feel sick, feverish. Am I coming down with the flu?*

I brushed off the discomfort and traveled on. But the closer I drew to the farm, the more severe the symptoms grew. My excitement took on a sense of foreboding. By the time I got to the driveway, my enthusiasm had turned to dread. Stricken with inexplicable fear, I lost my nerve and stopped the car.

*I can't do it. I can't go there.*

Rather than taking the drive that lay ahead of me, I veered off and continued down the road, past neighbor farms with their familiar houses, barns, horse pastures, and corn fields. I paused at the last driveway, took another deep breath, and turned the car around. My discomfort persisted as I drove past the farm drive. When I reached the state road and turned east, my uneasiness evaporated as quickly as it arrived. I aborted my mission and headed north to visit my friend in Chincoteague.

The following day was sunny, warm, and humid—a typical summer day on the Shore. It was a new day, though, and I was unwilling to ditch my quest altogether. I invited my host to join me on my second attempt to see the farmhouse. "Why don't you come along for the ride?"

"I think this is something you need to do yourself."

*Whoa. Wait a minute. Those were Jeffrey's exact words! What do they mean?*

This was no accident. It was a package neatly wrapped and delivered with care. I did not know what was in it, but I needed to figure it out.

Alone again, I retraced my steps and turned onto the county lane. Like before, a flush of discomfort overwhelmed me. I pulled the car over to the side of the road and, avoiding the ditches on both sides, made a three-point turn back to the intersection.

*What is happening inside me? What does this mean?*

It was irrational. But I needed to pay attention to the intuitive signs. I turned left this time, westward, towards the old crab house. Gram, Mom, and I had traveled there scores of times to pick up crab meat for chowder, fresh crabs for steaming, or soft shells for sautéing. All that remained there now were ruins. The complex was a shadow of its former self. Crabbing was less lucrative and more expensive than it had been when I was a child. Most of the crab men had moved on to find other work. Boats once carried crab traps to and from the Bay. They were gone as well, but the traps were still there, stacked on the docks and rusting at the water's edge. There were no ladies in the building across the way, where, dressed in gray uniforms, white aprons, and hairnets, they sat side by side at long, stainless-steel tables, chatting and picking meat from the steamed crustaceans. There was no one in the office to take our order for a pound of lump crabmeat, sold in white tins for five dollars a pound. In fact, there was no office at all; the building had been razed. All of it was just a fond memory. I stood outside my car, gazed towards the Bay, and let the memories wash over me to rinse away my dis-ease.

Back at my friend's fishing cottage, in the middle of the night, I was awakened from a sound sleep by a panic that came from deep within. A raging monster demanded release, and I was too afraid to meet it. This was not a simple nightmare. In fact, there was no nightmare at all. I had short-circuited it and woken myself before the dream could have its say. Shaken to my core, I trembled and wrenched. I was desperate to thrash away whatever was haunting me. I sat up, turned on the light, clutched the pillow to my gut, and tried to squash whatever it was back down into the dark depths of my psyche. I was not about to allow sleep to recapture me. I opened my laptop and played video games until dawn. The next day, I set off for home without ever making it to the farm.

✑

Three months after I squashed the incoming dream like a tarantula, a colleague invited me to fill her space as a speaker at a conference in Braunfels, Germany. The meeting for young people exploring their call to ministry was going to be held in this quaint village an hour northwest of Frankfurt. I was still unemployed and without prospects. I needed a change of scenery, so I accepted her invitation with joy and anticipation. A colleague in the German Methodist Church met me at the airport, and we drove through the pastoral countryside to our destination on the outskirts of the village. The twelve conference staff, organizers, and presenters gathered at the retreat center for introductions and dinner. We set the agenda for the next two days, and then, giving in to the burn from jetlag, I said goodnight and retired to my single suite in the dormitory wing.

I might have anticipated what would happen once I was untethered from the comforts of home. This was all unfamiliar to me, even the faces. I had left my job search at home, but I also left behind my defense strategy: my strong, fifty-plus-year-old fortress. And the monster still lay in wait.

In the dream, I walked towards a dark gray Cadillac. It was the one Dad had purchased and been so proud of when we lived in New Jersey. It was, for him, another symbol of his successful quest to achieve the American dream. The trunk of the car was open, and as I neared it, I could see inside. There lay the body of a young woman covered in blood. A man in a dark gray suit on the side of the car struggled to push the bloody body of another murdered young woman into the backseat. Both women wore 1950s-style, pastel gingham dresses. They both had wavy, dark, shoulder-length hair. I flashed back to pictures I had seen as a child. I knew them. These were my two half-sisters.

The man saw me approaching. His calculating, sinister gaze was familiar. I had seen it before. He dropped the corpse and started towards me. I was to be his next victim. He intended to get to me before I learned his truth. But it was too late—I already knew. I knew who they were. I knew who he was, too. And I knew what he had done. Not physical murder, but mental and emotional homicide. And subsequent abandonment, leaving his victims for dead.

The scene summoned memories of the night of my thirteenth birthday party when I stood up to him, but this time I did not speak. I turned and walked away. Unshaken and unafraid, I strode towards the rowhouses across the street where an older woman stood, clutching a handkerchief, on the steps of the first house. A brown caftan fell softly around her round figure. The lines on her ashen face and the panic in her eyes conveyed distress over what she had witnessed. She twisted the damp beige hanky, alternately wiping the sweat from her brow and the tears from her eyes.

I looked into her sad brown eyes and said, "Mi abuela, it's over. He won't hurt anyone else ever again."

She nodded, signaling relief, though I could see from her face she remained traumatized. In her powerlessness, she prayed his violence against the women in his life would stop. I squeezed her arm and calmly walked away from her and back into wakefulness. I shot up in bed. This was the nightmare I had repressed that night on the Shore. But this time, I was not afraid. Part of me was shattered by the realization Dad had perpetrated physical and emotional abuse on all three of his daughters. At a fundamental level, he killed us all. But the other part of me was relieved. The putrid toxin stagnating in my unconscious, coursing through every fiber of my existence, directing my life choices and behavior for decades, had at last wormed its way to the surface of my mind. At long last, I could begin to purge myself of the poison that had propelled my life. It was the worst dream of my life but also the best. I was free now. Liberated. Shackles loosed. Absolution poured over me like a bottle of sweet nard. I turned on the light and smiled.

On the long flight home from Germany, I dared to process the dream and began to realize the haunting questions were finding their answers.

*Why am I always in conflict?* Because of the unresolved anxiety rooted in my repressed memories.

*Where does my anger come from?* It is triggered by abuse, neglect, embarrassment, guilt, and shame from people and experiences that were never in my control.

*Why are you so sensitive?* Because I never felt heard. I had to listen to myself to stay sane amid the insanity.

*Why do you take things so personally?* Because I was abandoned and have not yet managed to heal the wound.

*Why do you rehearse every wound?* Because I cannot seem to find the root cause of the pain.

*Why can't you let things go?* Because as long as I hold them, I might be able to control the outcome.

It was as though I could hear the pins fall into place in order to open a safe. In an instant, it all came together. Everything made sense. I had opened the vault. The demons were released.

⁂

I thought the dream was all I needed to complete my healing. At last, I could put the past behind me. I did not know that recovery from early childhood trauma is not clean and straightforward. No one told me the body clings to it with the same vigor the conscience uses to repress it. The dream provided me with emotional freedom, but it was not to be mistaken for a complete redemption of the past. The dream tapped the tip of the iceberg. I had more work to do to find out what still lurked in the cold water below.

Back home, my body unleashed the secrets it had held for decades. Purple bruises, smaller than a dime, appeared on the inside of my thighs. Asthma returned with a vengeance. It did not attack me, but with every shallow, strained breath, it reminded me of the time Dad held a pillow over my face. Telltale discharge appeared. And the ubiquitous stench of stale cigarette smoke followed and haunted me.

Sharp memories came into focus, forming a picture resonating in my deepest parts. I read *The Body Keeps the Score* by Bessel Van de Kolk and understood my body was confirming my suspicions. Embellishing the answers to my questions. Though I did not have all the concrete details or solid memories of the past, for the first time, I knew my pain was not rooted in Dad's rage. My shame was not grounded in Gram's piety. It was the denied abuse which fueled my defensiveness and anger. The rejection I perceived as a child framed my self-protection and sensitized me to criticism. Mom's depression poured fuel on the fire. My anxiety and depression had a historical context deeper than having a "Latin temperament." I was not hungry or tired. I was abused and neglected. The diagnosis on the therapist's statement said: PTSD.

*It wasn't always about me. Maybe it was never about me at all.*

It was time for me to rein in the monsters of guilt and shame—the ones that had defined my entire existence. Still, I needed to acknowledge all the primary actors were gone. No one alive could confirm my stories or disabuse me of the memories that surfaced from the core of my being. I was on my own to interpret the history I was knitting together. No matter. Those memories were crystal clear and indisputable. They were authentic. Memory is a tricky thing. But when the body sends you confirmation, you know your mind cannot be far off. Trusting myself, I allowed other memories to surface until I finally had a pile of puzzle pieces to fit together to form a picture. I no longer looked dimly through a mirror, to paraphrase the Apostle Paul. I confronted my truth face to face. What I once knew, in part, I now understood more fully.

# CHAPTER 32

## Resilience

When I was in fifth grade, a bully pushed me to the ground on the playground. As he ran away, he stepped on my collarbone, breaking it and leaving me without the use of my left arm for six weeks. While my parents were busy handling the bully, my body was up to other things.

First, blood clotted around the site of the fracture. Then, my immune system triggered an inflammatory response, calling my soldiers in charge of repair to begin the healing process. Stem cells, marrow, and blood answered the call, migrating to my splintered bone. Calcium began to form around the edges of the break. Cells produced soft cartilage, which, over time, was replaced by more rigid callus. About three weeks later, new, healthy bone took over, and after six weeks, I was as good as new.

The dogwood tree on the west side of the farmhouse had not flowered in five years. In the fall, Gram was readying her garden for winter. She paused as she walked past the tree, and shaking her finger as if to chastise a small child, she said, "If you don't bloom in the spring, I will chop you down!"

The following spring, the tree produced one small, white flower on Easter Sunday morning.

On May 18, 1980, after two months of earthquakes and steam venting, Mount St. Helens exploded, unleashing hot lava and pulverized rock. The column of discharge rose fifteen miles into the atmosphere and dumped ash on eleven states. The force of the wind snapped off treetops in a split second. Fifty-seven people died, and the entire mountain was stripped of all life. Three months later, tiny green shoots began to emerge from the ashen landscape, sprouting from seeds brought in by wind and wings.

Nature heals itself. We do too, if we do not stand in our own way.

# CHAPTER 33

## Mo'okini, Hawaii Island

The sacred temple, Mo'okini Heiau, is now a massive ruin of basalt stones. It rises from a grassy plateau overlooking the Pacific Ocean on the northwest coast of the Big Island. The magnificent ocean views and occasional whale sightings betray its sordid past. According to legend, it was built around 480 AD by the high priest Kuamoo Mookini, exclusively for use by the ali'i nui, the high chiefs of the island. About five hundred years later, a priest from the South Pacific arrived on the Island. Pa'ao claimed the temple, ordered its walls to be raised from the original six feet to thirty feet, and dedicated it to the war god Ku. He called for it to be a site for human sacrifice. Men, women, and scores of children lost their lives to appease Ku. Over a thousand years later, visitors to the site still report experiencing an indescribable, unsettling energy.

Protection of and care for this sacred space has been passed down from Mookini to his descendants for generations. Today, High Priestess Leimomi Mo'okini Lum oversees the temple and its surrounding land. In 1978, she removed its restricted access and opened the grounds and temple to the public. In 1994, she dedicated the site to the children of the world. Today, visitors observe the Hawaiian custom of leaving a flower or a lei on the temple altar as a sign of respect.

In January 1999, Jeffrey took a class of Elon University students to study Hawaii's cultural diversity. Each subsequent year, he added more opportunities to provide students with a deeper understanding of the history and issues faced by island residents. In 2015, he added a visit to Mo'okini to the course.

Aunty Momi Lum greeted us in her living room overlooking the Heiau and the ocean. Her snow-white hair was pulled back into a bun. Her porcelain white robe disguised her figure, and her neckline was wrapped with rivers of purple and white plumeria. She channeled the energy of the past through her stories of the Heiau's history and her decision to dedicate it to the children. She was mesmerizing. The group of us sitting at her feet, college students, professors and their partners, were enthralled by her gentle fierceness.

After her talk, she ushered us down the hill toward the coast and invited us inside the perimeter of the stone walls. She instructed us to walk with mindfulness through the maze to its center. There, she called us to place the leis we had brought on the rough-hewn volcanic rock altar. "As you lay down your offering, leave what you need to leave behind. Not what you want to leave but what you need to leave. Lay it down. Leave it here." she said.

We stepped forward, one by one, each doing as we had been instructed. I had no clue what I needed to leave there. Nevertheless, I stepped forward and placed my lei with the others. As it settled on the altar, something mystical happened. An uninvited energy rose through my feet and rushed up my legs and torso into my neck and head, unleashing itself in a flood of tears. They were uncontrollable, and I had no idea where they were coming from. An ancient mystery gripped me and would not let me go. I could not stop this firehose, but I did not feel sad. These were not my tears. Somehow, though, I was aware of a powerful and mysterious release, a cleansing that was running its course.

# CHAPTER 34

# Northern Spain

Jeffrey and I marked our retirement in September 2018 by walking a portion of the Camino de Santiago in northern Spain. We signed up for what I called a "silver spoon tour," one where arrangements were made for our meals, comfortable lodging, and, most importantly, transportation of our baggage from one stop to the next. Together with a dozen other peregrinos, we walked the last eighty-five miles of the pilgrimage trail over nine days.

Pilgrims have taken this journey for centuries. Many who walk today do so with a personal motive or goal. Some walk for their spiritual growth. Others make the trek to mark a life transition or heal their grief. Some are avid hikers who travel around the world seeking adventure. Jeffrey was single-minded in his reason for walking: to solemnize the end of his teaching career and mark the beginning of a new chapter in his life. And though I, too, was newly retired, I did not have clarity in my reason for making this journey. I knew I was drawn to be there, called to go. Traveling to Spain with my daughter years before, I found a level of comfort in the country, at home among the people, the language, and the culture. This time, though, I was there without agenda, hope, or expectation. My simple, conscious desire was to push myself physically to see if I could walk eighty-five miles over nine days.

We met our group in Leon. All of the peregrinos were English speakers from America or Canada. Our guides were from Spain and fluent in English. They oriented us to what we could anticipate over the coming days. They provided "lockers," aka tote bags, for us to carry the few items needed each day for our walk.

As our orientation session came to a close, a fellow traveler raised her hand. "I heard this morning someone died on the Camino over the past weekend."

None of us wanted to hear it, but our guides confirmed it was true. Someone had begun his Camino with his son in southern France and died from cardiac arrest while crossing the Pyrenees. In an eerie way, it was life imitating art as portrayed in the 2010 movie *The Way*, starring Martin Sheen. In the film, his son began his pilgrimage in France and died in the mountains crossing into Spain.

The following morning, I checked my email at breakfast before we loaded our luggage into the van. There was a message from my former administrative assistant in Chapel Hill, a forwarded email from the consulting firm our campus ministry had partnered with to do some strategic planning. The company was informing all of its clients that its founder suffered a fatal heart attack the previous weekend while walking the Camino with his son. The news shocked me, but the timing and details inspired me.

My objective for walking the Camino was now clear—I dedicated my walk to this man, inviting his spirit to walk the Camino with mine. The strong sense of his presence surprised me. Some days, he was beside me. On other days, when it was sweltering, or the trail was quite steep and rocky, he was behind me, pushing me up the hill in the blazing heat of the midday sun. The next to last day, he gave me a shot of adrenaline and kicked me into high gear to rise above the exhaustion. I separated myself from the pack to hike the last few miles on my own, in silence, with him by my side. In Santiago, I had his Camino passport stamped, and I carried his certificate home with me, to deliver to his colleague and passed along to his wife.

That energetic presence heightened my awareness of the gift of the spirits who walk with us at different times in our lives. Sometimes, they come to serve us. Other times, we are offered the opportunity to help them complete their work. I wonder how often we fail to allow this kind of encounter to motivate us. Do we dare dwell fully in the presence of this mystery at all times and in all places?

# CHAPTER 35

A month or two before we left for Spain, my cell phone rang. Caller ID said, "Caller Unknown. Belle Haven, Virginia."

*A call from the Shore. Who could this be?*

I did not answer, holding fast to my rule to disregard calls from unidentified callers.

*Probably a politician wanting money.*

The caller left a kind, soft-spoken message. She had known Gram. But she did not say why she was calling.

*What could she want?*

Without a good reason to return her call, I deleted the message and forgot about it.

Two years later, she called again on a blistering August morning, the day after Thor's hammer had (not) slammed through our kitchen ceiling. My curiosity won out this time, and I picked up the phone.

Her sweet voice rang with the familiar Eastern Shore twang. I was still apprehensive, wondering why she was calling. I listened, expecting to hear clues of a potential scam. Her call was so unexpected I could not shake my speculation that she might be a fraud.

*Is she the embodiment of the truckers in my dream. Is she hoping to find a treasure?*

She sounded sincere as she described her relationship with Gram. "We met at church... When Emily stopped driving, I visited her on Sunday afternoons. I took her the church bulletin and a treat from fellowship hour. Your grandmother always greeted me with tea and her blonde brownies. She was my Bible teacher. She knew so much about the Bible."

I was hooked by her story but could not help but roll my eyes. Gram's theology was so different from mine, her biblical interpretation so opposite. To Gram, God was a human being, His word to be taken literally. For me, God had become an enigmatic energy, and scripture a guide for living. I was resisting her, but I knew it was Gram who I wanted to keep at arm's length.

Her adoration for Gram and the farm sounded genuine. Still, I wondered why she was calling.

*What does she want? What is her agenda? Why had Gram never mentioned her to me? Why had I never met her?*

As she spoke, I allowed long-forgotten memories to emerge from the darkness of my hole. Daffodils poked through the snow-covered ground of winter. Lilies of the Valley sprouted from the cold earth. Robins returned to the bird bath. Roses bloomed in Gram's garden once more.

I interrupted, "It sounds like you've been to the farm in recent days. Have you?"

"Oh yes. I go often. A couple from New Jersey owns it now. They hired my husband to oversee it when they are not there. We have become good friends. I go often to tend your grandfather's gravesite."

This was the opening I longed for. It had been nine years since my aborted attempt to see the farm. I mustered my courage. "Do you think I could stop by the farm sometime?"

"I'll be happy to ask, but I am sure he'll say 'yes.'"

Fourteen months passed, and COVID had essentially shut down the world, but on what should have been Mom's ninety-seventh birthday in 2020, Gram's friend met me under the picnic shelter behind the church where they first met. We wore protective masks, but the threat of illness was no deterrent to enjoying a beautiful fall day with bright sunshine and a gentle breeze. We exchanged stories and memories.

"Your grandmother gave me these," she said. She pulled from a basket a small bronze urn and a white and blue doily. I struggled to recall if I had ever seen them before.

She handed me a flat, white box. "She made the best brownies."

I opened it to find melt-in-your-mouth brown sugar butter bars. And the recipe. My heart swelled.

"If Gram could bake one last confection, I would have wanted it to be this."

I placed the tiny bit of buttery goodness in my mouth and was transported back in time to the dining room table at the farm. Gram, Gramps, and Mom were there. Love filled the room—and my heart.

We prayed together, gave one another "air hugs," and I walked to the car where Jeffrey waited patiently. I climbed beside him, and he pointed the car toward the farm. He was taking me home.

The fields we passed by were plowed under. The chicken farms appeared to be locked down preparing for winter. Waterfield's General Store, which once stood on the corner and served as the gathering spot for the small village, had collapsed in on itself, rotted beams and walls fallen on top of one another. The windows and doors of the church were boarded up. But the post office was the same—a tiny, one-room, white house with an American flag on a pole in the sandy parking lot. The pine forests were as I remembered them, ushering us along the county lane where I had been shut down twice before. This time, instead of feeling the onset of the flu, a surge of life-giving energy pulsed through my body. Excitement blew away all the residual discomfort.

The well-crafted sign at the end of the crushed-shell drive welcomed us to "Creek's End."

*Is this where my story ends?*

The old trumpet vines and the rusty, brittle, barbed-wire fence that once lined the driveway were gone, as was Gramps' hand-painted speed limit sign. Instead, nailed to a tree was this message:

NO TRESPASSING

Violators will be shot.

Survivors will be shot again.

"Lovely," I said to Jeffrey as he continued towards the house.

"So much for a warm welcome. Are you sure this is a good idea?"

"It's fine."

We drove on. I reimagined the fallow field on our right, and the days Gram and I walked among the corn rows there to pick a few ears to go with our steamed crabs at dinner. And the day we picked tomatoes. I lost a friendship ring among the vines and was shattered over the loss. But Gram retraced our steps and found it lying in the sandy soil.

I gasped when we rounded the bend—oxygen yanked out of my chest. Gramps' old tractor sat on the grass before me. It was worse for the wear. The rope around the steering wheel had disintegrated. The mowing platform had been removed. The engine cover was long gone. But so many memories connected to this old Farmall tractor were still intact.

We pulled up to the house and parked the car. When I put my feet on the ground, time stood still. I gulped the marsh air, and it took me back sixty-four years to that first visit.

We strolled through the gardens. "Gram's roses are gone, but this is beautiful. Hydrangeas, azaleas, camellias. And the pomegranate bush is still here!"

I peeked in the windows of the house. We walked past the three barns and the fig bush, now as large as the side of barn three. I paused at the tombstones and grave markers. I marveled at the pool and guest house. "I wish we'd had a pool back then."

On the dock, I inhaled the salt marsh air. It was low tide, just the way it was the day I first set foot on that holy ground. This day, though, the odor did not bother me. In fact, I barely noticed it. Gulls greeted us with their caws. I leaned over the edge, casting my shadow on a crab attached to the piling, dining on barnacles. My shadow startled him, and he waved his claw at me—like old times. I was filled with peace and joy—a profound peace that passed understanding. Gratitude washed over me—for the land, the water, and all this place had been to me. It was no longer mine but would forever be home to my heart and soul.

# CHAPTER 36

Signs of fall were swirling around outdoors, preparing me for the onset of winter. The sun was rising later and setting earlier. From my study, I watched the trees on the hillside shed their summer greens to take on shades of gold, burgundy, and auburn. Soon, the north winds would arrive and shake them all loose, stripping the trees and leaving them naked to endure the cold. I recognized it was all part of the process, but I still shuddered and reminded myself there is no new life without releasing the old one.

From the first asthma attack that landed me in the hospital at age five, autumn had always been a precarious season for my lungs. It often landed on cue as if to celebrate an anniversary. I was never sure if it was caused by leaf mold, the change in temperature, or returning to a classroom swarming with germs. Whatever the cause, it was a predictable vulnerability. I was grateful my adult body was more skilled at fighting off the symptoms than my younger self.

October 2021 was different. COVID had stolen the lives of millions around the world in nineteen months. Pharmaceutical companies had rushed to develop vaccines, secure FDA approval, and get shots into people's arms to save lives. People were finally emerging from their cocoons of self-imposed isolation, daring to venture back into the world. Jeffrey and I had navigated the pandemic without succumbing to it and had received two vaccines. So, I was caught off guard when a respiratory virus sidelined me. I tested negative for COVID twice before my doctor uttered the word I despised for decades because of the control it had over my life. Asthma. This time, I recognized it as a symptom of post-traumatic stress. The doctor prescribed a steroid inhaler. I went to bed for a couple of days, but three weeks later, I still struggled to recover. I pulled myself together and went for a massage.

"There is a truck on my chest all the time," I told my massage therapist.

I lay on the table, hopeful that my body would expunge whatever was ailing me. I attempted to will my mind into a dream-like state. Instead, my brain went into overdrive. An image of a plastic container floated from my midsection to my mind's eye. It was about six-by-six-by-six inches with a green plastic top like the one in my refrigerator storing mashed potatoes left from dinner the night before. This one bobbed past my eyes like a crab pot buoy in the Creek. Its top was skewed, and I caught a glimpse of the contents. Green fuzzy mold. Spotted with pink slime and crusty black chunks. It was the ugliest science experiment ever.

*It's past time to throw that out!*

I described the image to the massage therapist as we closed the session. "What do you think?"

"Ah, yes." She was careful in choosing her words. "There is something you need to say."

I sat in my car, my head against the steering wheel. I banged the wheel with my fists in full-throated resistance against what I knew I needed to do.

*I have nothing to say to him.*

Opposition and pushback were strong.

*Surely, there is someone else: anyone but him.*

I could not shake myself loose from what needed to be done. I wanted to find another target, but none presented the force and urgency he did. It was as if he was begging me to do it.

*Do it. Get it over with. You have held it too long.*

Back home, I knew what I had to do. I went straight to my study and settled into my black chair, with a pad and pen on the desk before me. I looked out of my office window at the hillside and took a few puffs from my inhaler.

*I lift my eyes to the hills from whence comes my help. Psalm 121.*

My air passages were open and ready to go. I was as grounded as I could be. There was no holding back. Tears welled up. Deep inhalations to expel the last bit of toxin, my life-long poison. I wrote of what led me to the truth. How my body kept the score. How my spirit was tortured. How determination to soar drove my resilience. How I managed to transcend a lifetime of suppressed pain. How one memory at a time pieced together formed a clear picture of early childhood trauma, abuse, and neglect.

Anger and grief poured out with every word. There was no sugar-coating. Nine pages later, I found relief. But as I reread it, I knew my work was not done. The letter needed an audience. I needed to read it aloud—to someone who could help me process it. No sooner did I have this thought when I noticed a neighbor walking in front of my house.

*She's a therapist. Maybe she can give me a good referral.*

Sarah's office was sparse. No pictures on the wall. A gray couch and chair. A small table next to her chair. It was an empty canvas waiting for the artist to show up. Who was the artist? Was it her? Or was it me? The offices of my previous therapists had been filled with fascinating distractions. They were warm, inviting spaces. Artwork on the walls. Soft cushions. Even tea to drink! This was different. It was an austere, sterile space. But I needed a good surgeon, not a cozy setting. Decades prior, a friend had advised me, "When you are seeking a therapist, know what you need." This time, I knew. I needed a therapist who would hear the letter, help me process it, and cut me loose to live a contented life. I was relieved not to have distractions to sift through. And I intended to give her everything she needed to help me finish this work.

"You should have known I would figure it all out one day," the letter began.

> You spent your life hiding the truth and thought you would take it to the grave. But it did not work. It did not protect you or me. You did not expect my psyche to uncover the pain and that my body would confirm my reality. But, instead, the truth prevailed.

I wrote about trying to return to the farm and the liberating dream. I listed the questions that had haunted me as a young mother, the unsolved mysteries that were still festering boils. I told him how the dream had uncovered the answers, addressing my life-long doubts and insecurities. All of the memories made sense now.

The wall of photos in the bedroom.
*I wasn't your princess, was I?*
My thumb-sucking until I was ten.
*We both know what that was about now, don't we?*
Relieving yourself in the bathroom when I was in the bathtub.
*You didn't think I noticed, did you?*
Bruises on the inside of my thighs embodied documentation.
*The final confirmation.*

The truth is, in the end, I do not know precisely what you did, or where, or when. I just know that you did. And I am better now.

A few weeks later, a dream that lasted only a few seconds completed the puzzle. Gram was standing in her rose garden when I approached her.

"Did you know?"

"Of course, I knew. We all did."

Still, it was hard to accept the truth. When I waffled, feeling the need to protect both the living and the dead, my therapist held me to account. "Why would a person who had not been abused make these stories up?"

She had a point and was not about to let me backslide.

At last, the family secret was out in the open, and I could get on with my life. But not before I reconciled something I had learned more than a decade earlier, something that still left me curious and unsettled.

First, the backstory. On the first day of Spanish class in middle school, the teacher asked if I spoke the language at home. When I told Señor Cataldo that I did not, he wondered why. Though the thought had never crossed my mind, suddenly I wondered too. That afternoon, I asked Mom about it. Her response stunned me.

"Your grandfather was a Venezuelan revolutionary during the years of the Gomez dictatorship. He was captured, he was executed, and your Dad and his mother fled the country with little more than the clothes on their backs. He was determined to leave his past behind, so he learned English and became an American citizen. By the time I met him, he spoke no Spanish. He barely even had an accent. He never spoke of his childhood or his homeland. He will not talk about it. We do not discuss it. Ever."

*Case closed.*

In 2005, Jeffrey and I took the ferry from Manhattan to Ellis Island. I delved into the database of the immigration records of men, women, and children who had traveled through those halls over decades, seeking a new life in America. I wanted to find the ship manifest that documented my father's migration into the country. Two entries popped up on the screen when I typed my father's name into the search engine. Confused, I poured over the two ship manifests, struggling to unravel the mystery. The first record was my father's, made clear by the presence of mi abuela's name on the line below his. Much to my surprise, the second manifest was my grandfather's, which I figured out by deciphering the name of the person he was coming to see: Maria Louisa Rivero, mi abuela.

I knew Dad and mi abuela had traveled to the U.S. from Venezuela by way of Cuba in May 1924. What was new and destabilizing information was that in September of the same year, another ship left Venezuela for Panama carrying mi abuelo, my grandfather. In Panama, he boarded another ship to New York, where he stayed ten days before returning home. Still, another manifest revealed that he had come through Ellis Island again two years later. On this second entry, the document indicated that he planned to stay for one month. If he sailed back to Venezuela a second time, there is no record of him having returned to America.

*Was he really a revolutionary? Was he really assassinated? Or was this another lie?*

I will never know. But the scrutiny of my search at least partially demythologized my father's story. He did not escape his homeland with the clothes on his back after his father's execution. The records revealed that he came to America as the son of a diplomat to attend a prestigious private school in New Jersey. Perhaps mi abuelo did return to his homeland and was executed. But when Dad came to America, his father was very much alive and provided my father with preferred immigration status. He was not the victim I always thought him to be. As I replayed all of those childhood memories with this information in mind, a clearer picture of who my father was began to emerge.

My life had been a dark room, but throughout the healing process, the pictures came into focus before my eyes. Snapshots from the past took on clarity as a photographic timeline of my father developed. I understood his lies as narcissism, maybe even sociopathy. Seeing him this way was painful but necessary. Another step in making the rough places plain.

In the spring of 2010, I reconnected with an old friend from my childhood over social media. Terry had lived a few houses up the street from me when we were kids. He was my first schoolgirl crush (after Paul McCartney). I had not been in touch with Terry for over fifty-five years. He was married with grown children and grandchildren and still lived in town. We exchanged a few messages. I mailed him some old pictures I had found of his garage band playing at a party in his basement. We realized through photos shared on Facebook that our families enjoyed the same lakes region in Maine. Then, in January of 2022, he sent me a message with a photograph. "Went for a walk today in our old neighborhood."

The picture was of the old California ranch house on Golf Street. The siding was beige now. The front door painted red. The copper beech tree Mom had planted still commanded the front yard.

*She would love to see the tree thriving.*

I was surprised to see the decrepit old pear tree, which should have died decades ago, still standing. It looked as pathetic as ever. The lush flower beds Mom had cultivated with such care, once dancing with daffodils, peonies, pansies, and Johnny jump-ups, had been replaced with uninspiring but easily tended evergreen shrubs.

The photo of barren trees and browned grass appeared ice cold, but it was January after all. The picture brought a vestige of a smile to my face. But the smile melted when I noticed my "thinking rock," the throne where I sat at the end of our driveway, was gone. That large granite boulder had been my grandstand seat to watch the cars pass by, while I wondered what was wrong with me. It was gone now—relegated to a landscaper's dumpster, I supposed. I had forgotten about that rock. My trusted, reliable friend. It vanished like a shadow that comes and goes with the sun. I paused.

*For keeping me sane. For being my rock. Thank you.*

A year later, Terry sent another message telling me the house had been razed. I gulped when the words slid off the page, but the photo he attached took me aback. A new house was under construction where the ranch house once stood. It had two stories, a frame under the roof, and walls without siding. There was symbolism in this new house, but I focused on what was gone.

"I hope you don't mind me passing along the news. I thought it was sad, but I'm a sentimental old fool," Terry's message said.

"The news jarred me, but it's better to know than to drive by sometime and see it. Thank you, truly. Thank you for letting me know."

*You are not a fool. Your message is a gift.*

My work was done. The book was closed. The urn, which once held the ashes of my childhood, had been demolished. Ashes to ashes. Dust to dust. The physical structure that framed the story of my trauma was no more. The walls and windows holding my ghosts were history, and the ghosts were set free.

# CHAPTER 37

Thanks to Gram's friend, I had reclaimed my connection to the farm. Thanks to Terry, I had absorbed the news and pictures of what had once been my childhood home. The words of Jesus came to mind. "It is finished." Then, a week later, I had this dream.

---

I am part of a team of videographers taping a documentary of ice skaters preparing for Olympic trials. During a break in our filming, I slip away to a nearby river beach. It is noontime, and the weather is pleasant for mid-April in New Jersey. The brilliant sunshine adds warmth to a gentle, southwest breeze. Walking along the riverbank, I take in the first signs of spring in the air. The river water is dark and smoky.

*What lurks beneath the surface?*

The squawk of a gull pierces the silence, letting me know I have disturbed his peace. The coarse gray sand crunches underneath my feet. I feel anxious, but not because I have interrupted the gull: I am searching for a film-worthy shot.

*What do I need to find? What needs to be recorded here?*

Then, as if on cue, it appears. Dropped from the sky. An answer to prayer.

*Ask, and you shall receive.*

A little girl is on the beach ahead of me, fifty yards or so away. Not wanting to miss the moment, I grab my camera to get her in view. The camera is rolling when I notice the film looks like the sand beneath my feet. It is gritty and grainy, with black specks. The film runs in jerky movements.

*This looks like an old family movie.*

The little girl looks to be about three years old, dressed in a blue and white pinafore dress. Her brown hair falls to her shoulders in unruly waves, with a white clip holding the tresses away from her face. She is not sitting, not kneeling. She is squatting—crouching to inspect the sand running through her tiny fingers.

*There are no shells here. There is no treasure to be scooped up and taken home. What is she looking for? What "pearl of great price" does she seek?*

I ponder these questions before realizing she is alone. There is no adult in sight. I look around to see no one is here to tend to her safety. Skeptical that this could be true, I pull my head back from behind the viewfinder, hoping to locate a supervisor in the bigger picture. There is no one. There is no one here to protect her. She and I are here, alone, together on the beach.

*Where are her parents? Who is watching her? No one is caring for her!*

I am alarmed. My stomach tenses. I am the only one who knows she is here. She has captured my imagination, my curiosity, and, most of all, my motherly protection. I want to film her up close, so I tiptoe towards her. She is laser-focused on the sand and seems oblivious to the reality that she is there alone. About twenty yards from her my epiphany comes.

*That's me! I am the three-year-old little girl, alone on the beach, sifting through the coarse sands of my life. And no one is looking after me. No one is caring for me. No one is protecting me.*

The camera slips from my hands and lands on the beach with a thud. I should care about the sand infiltrating its inner workings, but filming is no longer the point. I am not here to make a movie after all—not about her or Olympic skaters. I am here to see her. To watch her firsthand, in person. Not through a lens. I want to know why she is alone and searching for…

*Searching for what?*

Without warning, she looks up and sees me. She stands and breaks into a grin. She runs toward me, smiling the biggest smile I have ever seen. It is the smile of a child who has been found, one who is seen and known, as if for the first time. She leaps into my arms, throws her arms around my neck, and hugs me tight with the unfiltered enthusiasm of a three-year-old.

*I'll hide here, you come find me.*

It was never about playing hide-and-seek. It was about wanting to be found and needing to feel loved.

The Spirit of Mercy delivers a strong message that wells up within.

"Your job now, your only job, is to protect her and love her whole."

The sandy soil shielding her slips away. She emerges from her deep, dark fortress. I twirl her around, uncontrollable tears streaming down my face—a familiar river of tears.

*You are safe now, little one. You are home. You are loved.*

*For everything there is a season, and a time for every matter under heaven:*
*a time to be born, and a time to die;*
*a time to plant, and a time to pluck up what is planted;*
*a time to kill, and a time to heal;*
*a time to break down, and a time to build up;*
*a time to weep, and a time to laugh;*
*a time to mourn, and a time to dance;*
*a time to throw away stones, and a time to gather stones together;*
*a time to embrace, and a time to refrain from embracing;*
*a time to seek, and a time to lose;*
*a time to keep, and a time to throw away;*
*a time to tear, and a time to sew;*
*a time to keep silence, and a time to speak;*
*a time to love, and a time to hate;*
*a time for war, and a time for peace.*

*Ecclesiastes 3:1-8*

# BLONDE BROWNIES

## From the Kitchen of Emily Quinn

Melt over low heat one stick of butter. Remove from heat, stir in 1 packed cup of light brown sugar. Cool and stir in one egg. Sift in ½ cup flour, 1 teaspoon of baking powder, ¼ teaspoon salt. Add a ½ teaspoon vanilla, ½ cup coarsely chopped pecans, and ½ cup black walnuts. Spread in well-greased 8x8x2 pan and bake 20-25 minutes on 350. It appears soft when removed from oven but don't overcook because of this appearance. Cut into squares while it is still warm.

# GRATITUDES

The notion that "it takes a village" is never more accurate than the process of healing one's soul and telling one's story. The list of people to whom I owe great thanks is long and I am sure I will leave off someone. So, I ask forgiveness at the outset if I missed you. Please know that this book would not have been written without you.

For the encouragement to even start this, I owe a debt of gratitude to Jeanette Walls, whose story, *The Glass Castle*, and whose words, "Just write it," got my butt in the seat and my mind in the process; and to Barbara Brown Taylor, whose gentle presence gave me courage.

Profound thanks to the clergywomen who helped me jump-start the process: Kim Capps and Cindy Burkhert. To my critique partners Raka Chaki, Nancy Gilbert, and Cathy Osheim, and beta readers Kim Benton, Carrie West, Deborah Austin, Chris Bailey, and Sarah Holland for your multiple reads, critiques, seemingly endless input, and excellent feedback: thanks for helping to make it happen. Mega-props to Erin James, my warrior editor.

I am forever grateful to the professional practitioners who shepherded me along the way, even when I gave you nothing to work with: Pat Meyer Peterson, Joyce Forman, Betsy Wayland, Phyllis Koch-Sheras, and most of all, Sarah Lewis.

Extra kudos to Melissa Johnson, Sheree Bloch, Meg Lassiat, Terry Shea, Karla Kincannon and Gayle Shaw, who played significant roles while totally unaware. To Liz B. at Swem Library at William & Mary, who saved me from a citation crisis. And to the DFWUGs—you know who you are—who encouraged me.

Thanks to "Aunt" Edie Roberts for having the foresight to log the family genealogy for future generations. This never would have been written without those pages. Thank you for preserving the family connections so the third death has not yet come for the Swedish side.

To Michael Cheuk, who introduced me to Good Faith Media, and to the fine people there. CEO Mitch Randall; Carol Brown, author liaison, and Devin Harris-Davis, copy editor, both at Nurturing Faith Books, the publishing arm of Good Faith Media. Thanks to all of you for your expertise, assistance, and affirmation.

Nothing can substitute for the support of family. My life has been enriched by my extended one that includes Miriam, Benjamin, Anna, Campbell, Howie, Sam, Joy and Bizz. To my children, Kristen and Ryan: you have my heart forever. I love you to the moon and back a million times. I would not have done this had it not been for you. And I could not have done this without you, the one who forever props me up: Jeffrey, my partner, my rock. Thank you.

www.ingramcontent.com/pod-product-compliance
Lightning Source LLC
Chambersburg PA
CBHW070937180426
43192CB00039B/2312